So What If I'm a Puta

So What

THE FEMINIST PRESS
AT THE CITY UNIVERSITY OF NEW YORK
NEW YORK CITY

If I'm a Puta

Diaries of Transness, Sex Work, Desire

Amara Moira

Edited by
Amanda De Lisio

Translated by
Bruna Dantas Lobato
and **Amanda De Lisio**

Published in 2025 by the Feminist Press
at the City University of New York
The Graduate Center
365 Fifth Avenue, Suite 5406
New York, NY 10016

feministpress.org

First Feminist Press edition 2025

E se eu fosse puta copyright © 2016 by Amara Moira
Foreword copyright © 2025 by Charlotte Shane
Translation copyright © 2025 by Amanda De Lisio and Bruna Dantas Lobato
E se eu fosse puta was first published in 2016 by Hoo Editora, Brazil, and in 2023 by n-1 edições, Brazil

All rights reserved.

 This book is made possible by the New York State Council on the Arts with the support of the Office of the Governor and the New York State Legislature.

 This book is supported in part by an award from the National Endowment for the Arts.

This book is published with the support of the National Library Foundation of the Ministry of Culture of Brazil and the Guimarães Institute of the Ministry of Foreign Affairs of Brazil. Obra publicada com o apoio da Fundação Biblioteca Nacional, do Ministério da Cultura do Brasil, e do Instituto Guimarães Rosa, do Ministério das Relações Exteriores do Brasil.

No part of this book may be reproduced, used, or stored in any information retrieval system or transmitted in any form or by any means, electronic, mechanical, photocopying, recording, or otherwise, without prior written permission from the Feminist Press at the City University of New York, except in the case of brief quotations embodied in critical articles and reviews.

First printing July 2025

Cover design by Leila Register
Text design by Drew Stevens

Library of Congress Cataloging-in-Publication Data is available for this title.
ISBN 978-1-55861-348-5

PRINTED IN THE UNITED STATES OF AMERICA

And remember, Amara, Jesus said it first: "Prostitutes will get into the kingdom of God before you." (Matthew 21:31)

—MARIA VALÉRIA REZENDE,
nun and writer, three-time
winner of the Jabuti Prize

CONTENTS

Foreword by Charlotte Shane	ix
Introduction	1
01. Maybe One Day	11
02. The Beginning, Ah, The Beginning	15
03. Cruising Lessons	19
04. Little Girlfriend	23
05. Inflatable Doll	26
06. Today I'll Know Love	31
07. A Tranny to Date	32
08. A Different Kind of Sixty-Nine	39
09. Things Said Between Travestis	46
10. The OGs	47
11. On the Hood of the Car	49
12. My Porn Debut	52
13. On Top and Liking It	55
14. Freebie	58
15. Shitty Men Outdo Themselves	59
16. Today I Didn't Make a Mess	60
17. Radical Travestis	65
18. Men Will Be Men	66
19. Sometimes Shit Happens	68
20. Hate Bite	70
21. When It's Time to Do It, I Do It	73
22. What Do Sex Workers Want?	80

23.	This Puta is a Poet	82
24.	Escapades on Easter	84
25.	One Year of Amara, Two Levels of Fuck It	89
26.	Monologues of the Trash	92
27.	Object of Desire, Abject Body	95
28.	Now You've Earned Your Twenty	98
29.	The Minefield in the Bushes	102
30.	Oh, If There Were No Risks!	105
31.	Where's the Condom?	107
32.	Please Stop, I Came Here to Fuck	110
33.	Sex Under the Moonlight	113
34.	Yada Yada, Body Odor, In and Out	116
35.	You're Way Too Hot	119
36.	The Truck Motel	121
37.	Too Many Trucks for Too Little Sand	125
38.	A Puta in Europe	129
39.	Your Girlfriend for Fifty an Hour	133
40.	The Travesti's Sad Fate	135
41.	Possible Loves	137
42.	Sex Work and Free Love	140
43.	Not with That Lipstick	144
44.	If They Only Knew	147

Acknowledgments   149

FOREWORD
Charlotte Shane

I first met Amara Moira as perhaps you, too, will meet her: her makeup smudged, the taste of condoms on her tongue, riding the bus home as night leaks into morning. She introduces herself here through her first client: a motorcycle rider who paid her twenty reais for a blowjob, a man whose scent "made [her] mouth water." As their encounter unfolds, she is self-conscious, anxious, intensely aroused, and finally euphoric, back on the street and "still in shock" when her second client approaches her with fifteen bucks and abundant sweet talk. It's possible you will feel as disoriented and giddy as she; it's possible you will feel right at home.

Candor like Moira's cultivates a sense of intimacy between author and reader, but my immediate allegiance to her is also the result of decades spent in the company of countless sex workers, both cis and trans. Moira's life as a travesti, a Brazilian, and a woman who sells sex on the street is superficially not a life like mine (an American cis woman who has only worked indoors), yet much of what could be called "our story" is the same: the self-doubt and determination with which we took on the job, the revulsion and infatuation with the labor itself, and the parade of clients with big dicks, limp dicks, charming lines, bad breath, sad faces. Even the anal fissure earned and subsequently endured at work, we share. I feel a deep kinship with her, as I expect will many other putas, and (I hope) other feminists.

So What If I'm a Puta is a vibrant entry in the pantheon of sex-worker memoirs, those irresistible, incendiary documents that function as prurient entertainment, propaganda, detailed sexual histories, psychological profiles, and cultural anthropologies. Like the best of them, Moira's is marked by keen observations and bawdy self-deprecation. (Exemplified, for me, in the image of a stuck condom "hanging from me like a pony's tail with his load now dripping down my leg.") Her vignettes–revealing, titillating, and told with a generous sense of humor–make for excellent gossip, and I was desperate to share them with friends, screenshotting select passages to spur their reading. *So What If I'm a Puta* has many qualities to recommend it, and one of those is that it's great fun.

But undergirding the work is something more profound: a persistent ambivalence about her status as a puta, a woman, and a writer, and the relationship between the three. In this book's introduction, she describes herself as "a travesti who becomes a writer by being a puta, and a puta by playing a writer." The formulation is arresting, and it calls to mind another title in the sex-work canon, Melissa Gira Grant's *Playing the Whore*. For Moira, on this first page, the writer persona seems the more tenuous one and the puta truer; prostitution simultaneously makes writing possible for Moira and delegitimizes her status as one who writes.

Yet a few chapters later, an activist and would-be comrade praises Moira's blog as "good for the cause" despite Moira not being "a real puta." The apparently unintended insult hurts her terribly. "I grappled with loneliness and a longing to truly belong to the sex-worker community," Moira writes later, "to not be seen as a tourist." The categories we assume or are thrust into are both too tentative and tenacious for our fluid selves, and the ways those categories invalidate or reinforce one another are difficult to disentangle. What aspects of ourselves are indelible and which are performance? Do we answer this question for ourselves, or must we leave that verdict to an audience of potentially hostile strangers?

Similarly, selling sex has the power to make Moira (as it made me) feel affirmed in her womanhood, desired specifically *as a woman* and affirmed by her clients' lust. Before she earned her first twenty reais, she visited friends on the stroll and reveled in the harassment there, feeling "truly special" when men asked for her price. In this context, "they were allowed to desire my body," while elsewhere they would deny any attraction because of her transness.

But sex work introduces a new and equally insidious layer of stigma into her life. "I accepted you as a travesti, but I can't accept you as a puta," a (former) long-time friend tells her. In personal relationships as well as the broader world, Moira's status as a sex worker challenges those who think of themselves as open-minded, who are otherwise "empowered" in their love for and defense of queer and trans people. As Melissa Gira Grant writes in her aforementioned book, "sex work makes women who don't do it feel things they prefer not to feel." And sex-working women, like trans women, are regarded by reactionaries as corrupted, deceptive, or otherwise fraudulent women who selfishly endanger "real" (i.e., good) women with their depraved pursuits.

Because "whore" first and foremost indicates a woman

who has transgressed against respectability, "even [trans women] who manage to escape this life are still labeled putas," as Moira writes. When womanhood is made synonymous with sexual availability, anyone who claims womanhood has also, by definition, claimed licentiousness. This is hardly theoretical, though, and goes well beyond the realm of language. Transphobia drives trans people to the social margins, where prostitution greets them with open arms. Yet, as Moira writes, "putaphobia only deepens the exclusion we face." Then, too, there is the transmisogyny exacerbated by putaphobia, which compounds the risk that a man will turn violent at the first sign of rejection or denial. "When I transitioned," writes Moira, "I experienced sexual violence for the first time."

Moira's project is one of self-discovery or at least self-translation, self-articulation, which is also self-reclamation. Sex work allows her to access and express a part of herself that is otherwise out of reach, but writing may also be an excuse to continue with the work. "I don't quite know anymore if I am a sex worker to write or if I write to do sex work," she confesses. For another iconic feminist and prostitute, *King Kong Theory* author Virginie Despentes, writing and selling sex are twinned rebellions. Each requires "freeing oneself, doing what isn't done, delivering up one's intimacy, exposing oneself to widespread judgement, accepting one's exclusion from the group."

Moira adds another dimension to this relationship in her conclusion. "The stories protected me," she writes, referencing her paid dates and what she risked losing in the moment. The client's frame is society's frame, as is the man's frame, and the cis person's: for women, for trans people, for putas, it is others who determine our degraded worth. But because Moira was "always the narrator" of her experience, she retained a dignity and autonomy that might otherwise be stripped away.

Ultimately, her voice reminds me most of the French anarchist whore Grisélidis Réal, whose notes in her *Little Black Book* consist of reminders like "spit in his face when he comes in mouth" and who, early in a conversation with an interviewer, shares an anecdote of laboring hard for the orgasm of a customer who instead pisses in her mouth. Like Moira, Real is direct and descriptive to such an exacting degree that simple statements of fact are taken as provocations. Over the course of her long career, she is treated abominably, brutally, by the men who visit her, yet still she is capable of tenderness, kindness, and concern.

Moira, too, preserves her humanity in the face of the physical pain, disrespect, bad hygiene, and chaotic kissing to which she's subjected to by her clients. "Each one is human in his own way," she writes, "and I am interested in all of them." As are we, her readers, endlessly interested in her. We are lucky to be taken into her confidence, to watch and learn on the sidelines while she prods the quivering status quo and jabs its tyrants with her loving yet merciless "sharp pen."

–Charlotte Shane
Washington, DC
March 2025

So What If I'm a Puta

INTRODUCTION

Sitting on the bus on the way home, almost morning, a cold and empty night, phone in hands: This is how my story takes shape, gains color, comes to life. What I've just experienced still fresh in my mind: makeup smudged, the taste of condom in my mouth, my client's smell still on me, his manly smell so different from mine–is it the hormones? Certain words come to me as soon as I start writing: teeth, tongues, fingers, lips, one naturally grabbing the other, the words coming from our meeting but also from before, from when I stood on the streets, plotting love, playing nice: a travesti who becomes a writer by being a puta, and a puta by playing a writer.

There was no light, only smells in the bushes, and the many, many used condoms scattered on the ground making plopping sounds as we walked, looking for a quiet spot, me in my heels stepping on the soft earth, him–my first ever client–pushing the motorcycle. There was no light, but as soon as he pulled down his underwear there was a smell, sweat, the smell of a man, deep in my nostrils, making my mouth water. That is where we work, all of us, in whatever dark corner we can find–behind the avocado tree, or in the client's car when there is a car, or in a motel room or boarding house when they're willing to pay extra, and usually they aren't. Him on the motorcycle, he said he only had twenty reais in his wallet (he even opened it to show me)–just a blowjob, make it quick but nice.

I headed back out, still feeling self-conscious and uncertain about what to expect from myself, let alone from clients, nerves lingering from the first time. There's no class or book to teach you anything, nothing comes easy, it's all blood, sweat, and tears. Looking out of the corner of my eye with restless hands, wearing less than usual, a chill running through my body, my feet hurting from the heels, I stammered out my price, afraid I didn't look worth the amount. "How much?" Twenty reais, imagine! I was too rough around the edges, though maybe that was my charm, because in less than half an hour, several men stopped to talk to me, and this time, stuttering and all, I hooked one with ease. Fresh blood stands out, I was told. *Who the hell is the new travesti, the one in modest clothes?*

And there I went, unzipping the man's pants with that skill I'd forgotten to forget, my mouth searching for the base along the cock without ever even touching it with my teeth, my throat deep, choking, beyond the glottis. "Slow down, I'll cum like this," he said after just a few seconds, and then, "What a mouth!" The mouth of someone who does it with gusto, the mouth of someone who does it happily even with tears streaming down their face–imagine my surprise that I was aroused, my surprise at an erection in a member I considered dead. I'll admit, the strong smell did something to my sexual appetite, us in the dark, me nibbling, swallowing only his little head so he would last longer. Condoms for what? Who'd cast the first stone? He was to be one of many. I was so horny I couldn't stand it; he was paying in advance, and all I needed to do was what I already knew by heart from public restroom encounters, the dark corners of life. The difference was that now I was getting paid, finally getting paid, my great gifts recognized. For how much? Twenty reais—only a fraction of what this book is worth. But that didn't matter back then, and it doesn't matter now, because without those twenty reais I accepted that day, there would be no book today. It was those twenty reais that I was worth.

Half a year as Amara, and this man, this client, started to like me. He liked the trance I went into during a blowjob, me discovering sex, pleasure. But more than an orgasm, he wanted to kiss, and he asked me to. He brought me out of this trance to taste him on my lips and tell me how much of a woman he thought I was, how beautiful I was—everything I needed for my first steps as a true puta, my first steps as Amara. So I kissed his manly mouth, this man who didn't come close to matching the standard type (though my type was hardly a type as I desired the anonymity of it all, which was why I thought I'd make a good puta). I kissed him, and the next one, and the one after him, all of them. And this time, I didn't feel disgusted or dismayed by their manly mouths, foul breaths, bristly beards scratching my face: Being with men was so much easier now that I was a travesti, it all made me feel more like myself, more of a woman.

My dick swelled; my panties tightened like never before. There went the client looking for my body under my dress, pulling my panties to my thighs to see what I had getting harder under there, feeling up my ass but going through great lengths to dodge my dick, which I thought was funny. Then he led my face back down to his little head and came almost immediately, I did my best to hold back the urge to swallow: I made him pull out before he came and covered my face, my mouth still half open, hoping for a little taste, and he was delighted by the scene. He even took my number before leaving and made a point of calling me right then to make sure it was mine. He promised to be back, but I never saw him again.

In twenty minutes, if that, I was back on the street, euphoric, still in shock at what I'd just discovered in myself, this gift of making cash by giving pleasure: my first bit of cash on the street, finally a puta, feeling a job well done. Enough excitement for one night, I was thinking of maybe going home. I saw in my little mirror the liner smudged around my eye. I got cum on my face, what else? I fixed what I could, but I barely got situated before a car stopped, the guy wanting whatever he could get, everything he could get, for the fifteen reais he had in his pocket.

"Pretty face, feminine, and sweet on top of that. You kiss too? Then do it for me for fifteen, come on . . . I'll take good care of you; I know what you need."

I liked him flirting with me like that, my hair still short–the first few times I allowed myself to go out without a wig, no mane. I told him I was practically a virgin, first day on the streets. He said okay, and I agreed to the experience. I climbed into his car, and we went to the vacant lot, and right away I put my hand on his groin to size up his package. Huge cock, thick as a log: I exercised all the muscles in my mouth so I could go as deep as possible without my teeth getting in the way (no condom again, I didn't even try to ask this time). A fresh soap smell wafted from his cock, recently washed; that was the only thing that upset me, I'm a sucker for that smell of manly sweat. It was still worth it, though, and I gave it my all, but he wanted more. He wanted to fuck, and I was dying to find out if I could, so I let him. We got out of the car, everything moving along now, me lying with my back on the hood, my legs wrapping around his body, right out in the open, other people doing the same only a few meters away. Lube, condom, finger, more lube, push, push, but it wouldn't go in, it just wouldn't. His wasn't made for assholes, I thought, though I'd soon find out his wouldn't even be the biggest one of the night.

Understanding the situation, he took off the condom and I sucked and touched him until he came, half on my face and half in my mouth, but not before he sucked me too. I was terribly horny again. I promised to make more room next time, and he promised to come back. He said goodbye with a peck on my lips (I forgot to say how much we kissed, how affectionate he was), leaving me in the dark, among the bushes, wiping my smeared face and asshole with pieces of toilet paper. He gave me the fifteen reais as soon as I got in the car, before I even had to ask. Easy-peasy.

The third one, he was different. We'd met before, him all over my good-girl act (Travesti Nun was the nickname he gave me because of my modest clothes). He got my number and called some fifteen times before I finally picked up; he was crazy about me without me even lifting a finger. I had to turn off my phone while I worked with the other clients that night; that's how persistent he was. I got rid of the second guy, slapped on some makeup, and ran to where he was, some kind of boarding house, a makeshift motel. He was at the door with a beer in his hand and offered me a sip from his own can, which I declined. He wanted to make conversation, hear about my boyfriend (I know that trick!)–if he gets pissed off about my job (good one!), about my first day on the street. I played along, acting all innocent, and soon he took the opportunity to ask me to be his girlfriend, the first of I don't know how many requests–"Oh, but we just met, honey." Bullshit on top of bullshit, we only moved on because I finally asked, annoyed, if I could do my job already or what!?

"Sure, all right, do you want to go to the bedroom?"

"That would be nice, but we haven't discussed the price yet."

"How much?"

"Forty."

I tried the boyfriend angle with him, as we call it on the street, and the act lasted for more than an hour. He's the only client whose name I remember (we went out several times after that), the only one who never haggled the price or belittled my work ("The poorer they are, the more respect they have for us . . . I had one come every month counting his coins, never asking for a discount," a friend said when I told her this). As soon as he turned the key to lock the door, he took off my clothes and jumped on top. Stale beer breath, but I didn't mind because it was there, in this bricklayer's arms, that I was learning to feel like a woman, to hug and kiss as a woman. His tongue made me his, invaded my mouth, rough hands running all over my body. I quietly let him feel in control, enjoying this pleasure that had been foreign to me until now.

We lay on the bed, arms and legs intertwined, completely naked; free from hierarchies, from control, from getting ahead of ourselves or trying to finish first. He didn't want to have anything to do with my cock, though it was plenty hard. He was only interested in the female me: my breasts, which he hungrily caressed with his mouth and calloused hands; my ass, too, he fervently fondled my tight asshole with his fingers. I followed his lead, groping the volume in his jeans, shivering all over just imagining his cock inside me, thinking of how I struggled with even the smaller one before!

Oh, how I suffered–suffered so much. But before that, an overwhelming desire consumed me, an incredible horniness. That manly smell coming from his cock, him playing with the limits of my throat, my eyes watering, my nose running, me careful not to gag up my lunch– is there anything better than this? If up to me, I'd have stayed there forever in bliss (the next day my throat would be sore, a sign that I went too hard)–but of course he wanted more. I told him this was my first time in over a year, desire and fear in my eyes; he promised he would take it easy, and off we went.

I lay face down on the bed with his tongue in my ass, the taste of lube from the earlier attempt maybe exposing my truth (like there was time to take a shower, you think I'm paid enough for that?). If that's what he thought, he didn't show it at all. He seemed to be having a damn good time, and I was too. Once his tongue had enough, he pleaded sweetly to me, wanting to rub his dick on my asshole without a condom, infamously "just at the door," "just the tip." You know, men. An emphatic "no" from me was enough for him not to insist.

I opened the free packet of lube from the clinic to carefully grease the place he would go in and then started putting his dong in the condom that came with the lube. But who said it would fit? I called the other dick from before a log, but this was the first time in my life I'd ever see one not fit a condom . . . imagine my desperation: me, an inexperienced prude. Maybe he was used to it; he quickly grabbed his dick, and with two fingers on each side of the condom ring he stretched it wide, unfurling it along his blessed limb. Imagine me watching this scene, in awe . . . either the condom would rip, or my asshole would, there were only two options.

(A year and a half later, imagine my shock: the pain I felt every single time I had sex after that night was because of an anal fissure! It took me a long time to realize that I needed a doctor. I kept thinking I was just weak, or needed more practice, so I let in dick after dick, making matters worse. Two months of prescription ointment, three daily applications, and it got better, but I almost ended up on the operating table. Almost. As I said before, there's no class or manual to teach you these things; not even the doctors quite knew what to say.)

Back to where we were: me face down with my legs splayed like a rotisserie chicken, him on top of me. The only light was coming through the window, just enough for us to distinguish our bodies. And he put that big head inside me, and started pushing his way in, negotiating every painful inch with me. Many, many different positions, all terribly painful, maybe because the earlier attempt had already lacerated me, but eventually he got in. And when he got in, then yes, he could finally start to thrust with pleasure, and I just let him take my body, go ahead, do whatever you want, proving to myself that I could handle it: horniness, I mean, my own, another's. I didn't have a boner anymore, only pain, a lot of it, and the will to get through it.

At some point, he finally noticed me wincing in pain, and stopped. He took off the condom and let me get back to what I do best, sucking, swallowing. A glorious idea, it even got me aroused again (and again now, as I write this, how obsessed I am!). Between blowjobs and handjobs he finally blew his load on my face. I playfully licked up his milk with the tip of my tongue–oh my Lord! We started to get dressed, he continued to be super affectionate as I moved in a haze, unsure of the best way to ask for my money, when he spontaneously offered me fifty reais without even a word from me. And when he saw me pretending to look for change (putas never have change, I would soon learn), he gestured for me not to worry. We said our goodbyes, and I went out to tell the world.

No specific type, each one excited me. Giving pleasure was my bitter fate. Yes! Giving, but also receiving. If getting pleasure from work is a key factor in choosing a career, then mine was already chosen. So what if I'm a puta? Well, I am now.

01.
MAYBE ONE DAY

"I liked walking with my eyes on the ground, watching my feet, avoiding the stares of others. That way, I didn't have to wonder what they might be thinking when they saw me. If they laugh, I try as hard as I can to believe they are laughing at some joke or something funny they've just remembered. I put myself in this rosy little world, one that protects me. I don't glance back, I don't return all their looks, I just keep walking, oblivious to everything around me. And I manage to make myself believe, for the most part, that these outbursts of laughter or abrupt nods have nothing to do with me. I can quickly come up with some excuse, something I can cling to without much effort. But there are times when the laughter aligns too closely with my passing by, and I'll be hurt. And there are times, in these moments of insecurity, when someone who likes me, who I like too, will see this happen and ask me how I stand it, how I manage not to spit in the faces of those miserable people. I manage by playing dumb, that is how. Because if I pay any mind to what is going on around me, to how people are looking at me, to how little sense I make to them, I will have to lock myself in my room and cry. Like yesterday. At these moments, I find myself fantasizing about the times I'd visit my puta friends at work, how I felt truly special when the men openly harassed me, asking me for my price and looking at me with eyes full of lust, talking to me, flirting with me, catcalling me, trying to seduce me like I was the last Coca-Cola in the desert. I never gave in to these crude attempts, but the smile on my lips was enough for the men to see I didn't exactly hate them either. To be an object of desire here, an object of ridicule there, a mere object either way. But at least those puta-seeking men put me on a pedestal, made me feel worthy of admiration and desire. I don't really know why I keep letting this silly moralism keep me from making the right decision for myself."

Bitter Fate, Amara Moira: This is who you are, this is what it means. A name, my name, but no one says it. Melodious, maybe friendly, like the face I make when someone asks me for a quick blowjob for ten, or full service for twenty. Dealing with johns is something you hear about all the time, I learned right away. A travesti in her thirties pretending to be in her twenties, an LGBT activist, a feminist, a writer, a doctoral student in literary theory at the prestigious University of Campinas in her spare time, and a puta. "And a puta?" But why? "What do you mean, why?" I am a puta because I am a puta, a puta because maybe one day. Have you ever seen a trans woman as a teacher, lawyer, scientist, doctor? They want me to be the first; they want a little piece of paper, a doctorate, to open the doors of the world for me, the only one, the different one: "Come, Amarinha, work with us, we want you so much!" And telemarketing, beauty salons? I would rather be a puta! I prefer that to hearing insults eight hours a day—on the phone, doing nails or hair for a lady with a king complex.

So many years putting off my transition, in the closet, afraid to even tiptoe outside. What was I afraid of?

Everything. But above all, afraid I'd have to work sex, that suddenly, overnight, out of nowhere, sex work would be my only option for earning a living. The nameless bodies, various, varied, atypical, in varying degrees of hygiene and beauty, none of that scared me. I was fine with them and even preferred it that way, anonymous, atypical (the way I had always felt, especially now). The sex itself was easy, even the most eccentric kind: What was difficult was to make love, to combine love with pleasure. What really scared me was the violence of exclusion, the possibility of suddenly seeing myself as an outcast, being treated like garbage, losing my family, my friends, my social circle, losing the roof over my head, the right to continue studying, to be able to get a job, and to be recognized as other than a puta.

But there I was, two years ago, a travesti at last. Who knows what came over me, where I found the courage after only a few months of hormone therapy, my body neither here nor there, half and half, loneliness eating me up inside. I was dying to be touched, to hear "You're so beautiful," "You make me horny," yet nothing. Awkward, afraid to let anyone get close, but every time I visited my friends on the streets, there was no way around it. I got showered with "How much do you charge?" "I want you," "You're hot," "Just say how much," me getting wetter with each proposition. Men. They were allowed to desire my body there, on those streets; only on those streets could they come out of the shadows.

My more experienced puta friends, who'd been fighting this fight for years, started to encourage me to give it a try. I felt their suggestion had an imbedded warning–"You can't just come here to be a tourist"–or the idea that this was something I had to do for real, maybe it was just an alibi to throw myself into it. The question of "What if I were a puta?" started to devour me; a desire to defy the night with my little hormone-filled breasts, my hair still short, me still an apprentice in the art of seduction. Now I was already someone else, and I was willing to pay the price–that is, to demand it; to earn for all I knew I could learn, for the fiery desire that was mine to provoke.

So, two different ways of saying "fuck it": Not only would I become a puta, but I'd also tell everyone about it. I'd shout my profession, I'd write about the streets as I saw them, as I lived them, as they became mine, as they discovered my body alongside me, as I became free.

02.
THE BEGINNING, AH, THE BEGINNING

All that excitement I told you about, those electric first encounters–well, that didn't actually happen right away. There was a day before that day; a day that I sometimes wished to forget. After more than a month of me wondering "So what if I was a puta," friends were shocked to learn I'd ever thought about it. They tried to convince me that it wasn't a good idea; one even ended our friendship at the mere mention of the thought keeping me up at night. Seven years of friendship and all it took was for me to admit that "I was thinking of giving it a shot" for her to throw it away. I could already feel the weight of the stigma–"I accepted you as a travesti, but I can't accept you as a puta"; "You're going to get AIDS, get raped, there's no way, bye"–but no one understood that the choice was already made. I had already made my decision. By that point, I was focused only on the details, the things I would say, the weak excuses I would give. My life was already weighed down by shame. Feeling disgusted for desiring men, trapped by my own cravings, I ended up sleeping with anyone who would have me as long as they remained anonymous–regardless of dick size, weight, height, or level of beauty. Then, suddenly, I realized that this might be the only profession where, as a travesti, I would have easy access. I was treated like a whore long before I came out as one–almost as if there was a mark on my forehead. All they had to do was see me as a travesti, and the harassment began—harassment I had never encountered while posing as a man.

The beginning—ah, the beginning. My first actual day on the street, cars and more cars passed me by, my eyes awkwardly trying to meet those of the drivers as I tried to entice them with a word, a gesture, a finger on my lips, a wink (more like a grimace), trying as clumsiness oozed from my pores. At one point, a friend saw me getting desperate, struggling to land a man, so she took me into her closet and lent me an outfit more suitable for the job: a dress that barely covered my panties! You can imagine my embarrassment. I went back to the street and everything stayed the same because in this job, confidence is everything, precisely what I lacked. Clients need to be able to take one quick look at you and feel like you are what they need, what they're looking for, what will make them cum like crazy—otherwise they'll go after someone else. That's why it's important to play big, to know how to stir up a client's desire even when you're feeling small, even when you want to strangle the bastard. Clothes are the least important part of the job, everyone in the business knows this, but my friend insisted I change into something nicer to see if my axé (my luck) would come. But it didn't; I still struggled.

Quickly, I realized that providing this service—sex, intimate contact, time with my body—was easier in theory than it was in practice: How much was my time worth, my body? Saying X amount meant hearing "X minus Y," and the bargaining chewed away at my self-esteem. Five hours balancing on high heels, colder than I thought possible, going from corner to corner every hour to see if my luck would change, staying away from the others so I could stand out: Who was I next to those beautiful bodies? What chance did I have?

One man showed interest in me, his nose bleeding from all the blow he snorted, but he wanted the full service in the back of his car for twenty! That offer gave me chills, but even if he paid me twice as much, three times, I would have still felt insulted, given the situation, given the treatment. My puta friends would say, "Better twenty in your purse than in the purse of another because there's always someone who will take the money." But I don't know, maybe I came here from Neverland, because that bloody nose, those bulging eyes, the way he talked to me, everything made me panic. Plus, I feared he might say in the end that this wasn't worth it, that I didn't deserve the twenty.

I put my foot down: "I won't do it for less than thirty." Only ten more, big difference. I was quietly hoping he'd decline, which he ended up doing, but not without badgering me first. It was my "virginity" at stake, and I wanted to feel like more than a hole, more than the awkward and ugly puta this clueless fuck saw me as and thought he could have for cheap. And so I turned him down, the only concrete offer I received in five hours as I stood there on my first day, making eyes at the passersby.

Nighttime wasn't great, so I was later told: The early hours of the morning were best. But my clothes weren't warm enough, I'd just recently recovered from the flu, and my self-esteem was so low. No way I could face all that for several more hours. The high heels pinched my feet, and all I wanted was to feel the warmth of my own bed. I ended up crying the whole way home, thinking that I wasn't good enough to even be a puta, an ugly whore, less than cannon fodder, of so little worth. A lot of friends helped me cope with this trauma. We smoked a lot of grass, and drank a lot of booze, before I was finally able to try it again, exactly one month later: That's the night I shared with you at first, to hook you; I'm no fool.

03.
CRUISING LESSONS

My sexual orientation was somewhere between uncertain and unstable, often both at the same time. I was unable to love anyone, and therefore unable to have relationships, for long stretches of time; I ended up having a lot of partners in rotation, no wonder I thought I'd be good at turning tricks . . . (11/18/2004)

Diary open, I'm traveling back ten years. It's a shame I wrote so little back then; in one hour I read all the pages of a story I'd forgotten long ago. Things that I'd buried deep in my memory; I hardly know how I managed to submerge them so well if I did really experience them! Maybe my memory had played tricks on me, or maybe I was prone to seeing myself as a kind of character and dissociating . . . all I know is that I got a great deal of pleasure from realizing, at a young age, that it was a waste of both time and money not to charge for something I did so well. I used masculine pronouns for myself in my writing because, at nineteen years old, it was hard for me to see who I really was. I read in my diary all the spicy descriptions of my first few public restroom encounters, the silent exchanges and glances in the mirror signaling what would happen next.

Everyone who frequents the men's room knows men don't make eye contact in there; they don't talk, they don't say hi, unless they're trying to start something. I very quickly learned the silent language of cruising, of starting something. The bathroom was empty, I had it all to myself. A few people came in, and I took my time washing my hands, discreetly trying to find a look that might reciprocate mine (and you really can't be too careful doing so, there's no shortage of macho men willing to break your teeth if they feel uncomfortable). Then I noticed a guy standing for too long at the urinal ("Wow, what a tireless bladder!" someone more innocent might have thought). He looked at me out of the corner of his eye, trying to read me. It didn't take long for us to figure out what each other wanted; having washed my hands for a long time, fussed with my hair, checked my teeth, I finally went back to stand next to him to pee despite the row of empty urinals. Nearly on top of him now, I could easily size him up, touch him, play with him for a moment, before we went to the farthest stall, where I immediately sat on the toilet and lowered his pants.

There's no talking, no affection, and I don't even need to ask him not to touch my dick: It is his dick that matters; his and his alone. Pulling down his underwear and only then discovering the flavors and aromas that await me, thanking him for the opportunity to please a real man, a straight man. You can go in hard, of course, that's what I'm here for. Actually, I would love if you came without warning so I choke—so I can cough up your cum with a naughty smile on my lips, can you imagine? A shame this doesn't happen more often. Once my job is done, I show him that I swallowed it all (it's wrong to let cum go to waste in these circles), and thank him one more time, his indifference reminding me that I did nothing more than my job. Oh, and after that, if I run into him in the

shopping aisles–the best cruising happens in the mall–
holding hands with his wife, their children by his side, he
will pretend not to know me, fully trusting I would not
commit any indiscretion. This is the code that all those
who dedicate themselves to the practice follow.

Take a look at this little prose poem of mine from at
least fifteen years ago, really bad and, for that reason,
still unpublished today, but very revealing of my obsession with bathroom cruising (mixed with another of my
obsessions: making puns):

To Give/Forgive
*the nameless queen salivates for the fly that opens and
with a touch of the tongue to the dick, they're joined
as one. the cock fills her whole mouth, seeing blindly
through skin: inside it hesitates, exalts the return
when outside; then it turns over, devoured by the life
it unleashes. he says goodbye, then, and looks at the
queen with disgust: cum in her mouth, finishing her
handjob. both leave through the door, now open.*

Cruising is one of the few things that I miss from before
I was Amara. I loved feeling that unbearable, uncontrollable pleasure, my wiener soft . . . my desire didn't
live there, it was all in my head. It was horrible, but also
wonderful, hard to explain. How much easier would it
be if we could control our desires? Then we'd dutifully
want missionary and everyone would be satisfied, happy.
Or not. At any rate, it was by reading my old diaries and
poems that I realized that I was and had always been
a puta. Not necessarily the kind who charges for sex,
because at the time I didn't even know that was possible. But the kind who always had lots of sex, with lots

of different people, always with great pleasure. If having a lot of sex meant being a puta, then I'd always been a puta. Now I just needed to learn how to get paid for it, because even at the tender age of nineteen, I already knew I was a pro.

04.
LITTLE GIRLFRIEND

"I've been looking for you for so long, you're hard to find, you know?" A client who readily falls in love with the whore who acknowledges him; him, the one who called me a nun because of my modest clothes, who asked me to be his girlfriend after just one kiss. He fell for me, and now he refuses to leave me alone. I took a trip to the interior of São Paulo for a political event and ended up in the town where he lived, so he jumped at the opportunity to get with me, poor me, impaled alive (by his big dick)! News had spread throughout the event that I was writing a blog about my experiences on the street, to the point that an important activist came up to me cheerily to say the blog might actually be good for the cause, even if I wasn't a real puta. Now, who wasn't a real puta? I can't tell you how much that stung. Some people thought I was doing sex work to be political, for the activism—to be fair, I am partially to blame for their believing that—but her stripping me of my authenticity was a low blow. So I made a point of arranging to meet this obsessed client in the front lobby of the hotel where the event took place, and I was lucky that he arrived while everyone was there, including this "big-time" activist.

The hunk—he was hunky—got out of his cab and greeted me with a kiss on the cheek, as we got incredulous looks from the other attendees. Then we headed to bumfuck nowhere; I kept wondering what I'd gotten myself into, and if I would ever come out of there alive. But I calmed down once we arrived at the motel, and I got loose, undoing his belt, kissing, making out. I'm all yours, come here, you'll see what I'll do. He liked it, and I was already in my element, ready to do what I knew best, little girlfriend style: "Give me a hug," "I've missed your body." I took off his pants, and out flooded that masculine scent that made me crazy, made me salivate and then lick and then swallow and you know very well what. Another round of making out, my dick hard from the start (I really am good at this); it piqued his interest, he played with it a little bit, something he hadn't done before, and I, naughty, asked him if he wanted to switch roles that day. Hah! No way, not with him; he showed me who was in charge. He spread my legs open, grabbed the lube packet, and with his finger went in and out, his cock hard with the condom already on, then he tried putting it in and it hurt, it hurt, it hurt, even after he'd pulled out, the pain didn't go away. But he kept trying until he got all the way in, master of his domain. He started out slowly, getting excited little by little, then began to thrust steadily and confidently. And right as I was about to pass out, helpless in his hands, he went even deeper, again, again, one more time, and then he stopped, phew, and threw his tired hunk body on top of mine. We kissed, he pulled out, the condom covered in evidence (I didn't yet know how to douche!). Wow, that was so good; I love going out with you; just wait, there will be more. We took a shower, then he called a cab, the two of us cuddling in bed as we waited. I wasn't even sure how to charge him because we hadn't agreed on a price beforehand. Finally, I worked up the nerve to ask, "What about my share, love?"

"Oh, right. How much is it again?"

"The usual."

And so he added a crisp fifty reais to my collection. He accompanied me back to the hotel, and as soon as I arrived, I ran to the club with my girlfriends to spend my pay. Easy come, easy go.

05.
INFLATABLE DOLL

No kissing, no "Come give me a hug" or even "I like you": This time I was just a mouth, an ass, a body, and nothing more. Being used the way I'd always dreamed of, but I didn't exactly like it as much as I thought I would. "A blowie for ten, do you accept?" It was already a shitty night, freezing cold, I wanted to get into a car as soon as I could (being in a car was already a bonus, an improvement from the streets). "So do you accept?" Yeah, of course, but I play hard to get too. Our session began, I pulled down his pants and underwear and grabbed his dick; it didn't smell so clean. I sucked it off and got it up, I was really good, and then felt his hand move up my spine, grabbing my curls. Was he being affectionate? He was not: He grabbed my head and pushed in his meat. I choked, I felt like vomiting, I held his hand so I wouldn't puke, the way I usually like it, but I didn't at all this time . . . and I didn't know why.

Maybe it was because he was this rough guy in a Mancha jersey, blatantly belittling me ("Do it for ten, I won't pay more than ten," and then "Do you have change for twenty?" and me, such a sucker, offering him seven). It was a very tense situation, three hours standing outside in the cold and not a single client to warm up the night; there I was, vulnerable, feeling ugly. It wasn't how I pictured my return to the streets. But it would get even worse: "For fifteen, can I get the full service?" Seriously, for two more bucks he wanted the whole thing, right there in his car, squished in the back seat, and I didn't even like taking it in the ass that much. Unacceptable. So finally: "No, and your time is running out." Annoyed, I did what I could to get it over with, and he, pissed off that I didn't accept his offer, came without giving me a heads up. The bitter wind hit me again when I opened the car door to spit out the jizz, and despite the cold, I wanted to get out of the car as soon as possible. Once that was done, with thirteen bucks in my pocket, I could at least cover my expenses for the night, the bus fare there and back, dinner, and catch a glimpse of the hundred I'd planned to earn that night.

What's funny is that nowadays, rereading this story, his abuse titillates me, and I am left wondering if I couldn't have found a way to enjoy it more at the time. It's not uncommon for me to walk away from guys who cross my lines, to curse them and their mothers, only for me to go out with them again or get turned on when I remember them. My first sexual relationships with men were like that, and I'm still annoyed that I get horny when I think of the piece of shit who took my anal virginity. Would I like it to be different? It would be nice if I felt that way, but it's not entirely up to me, and I don't want to lie here, to pretend reality is prettier than it is.

Digressions aside, I went back to my post, and soon another piece of shit showed up. He came up close to me, lowered his car window, and I said, almost on autopilot:

"Looking to get some love, baby?"

"What do you think?"

"I think you are, and I'll say more: I think you're looking for me."

"I am. There's just one problem . . ."

There we go again. The sorry fucker left his house with nothing, maybe he forgot his wallet, maybe he was scared he'd get mugged, turned out he only had eleven in change from the tollbooth–could I maybe get some head action? Fuck, they love to pretend this isn't a job for me . . . They can't do without our services but insist on devaluing our labor so they can pay us less. That's what all that talk– "They don't want to work," "They do it because they like it"–achieves: It reduces the worth of an essential service in a patriarchal society. In moments like this, I can almost understand why underselling is discouraged and disliked by other travestis: If one sells something for less, then there's pressure on others to do the same, or to accept less as the new standard, you know?

It's like I only attract stingy men! At least this one treated me well and tried to please me, but I was worried I wouldn't be able to afford my basic needs (the cold was already gnawing at my bones again), so in a moment of desperation, I accepted his lowball offer. I did it–full service for a wholesale price–much to my colleagues' horror. Naturally, this was the first client I couldn't get hard, no matter how hard I tried. I tried everything: I sucked slow, fast, steady, gentle, deep, just the tip. I sent my tongue in useless twirls, used all my throat and lip skills, and still, he only managed a semi. He apologized, thanked me for my commitment, blamed it on the booze before taking a hit of coke. "I barely feel it, but it gets in the way," he said.

When he said the word "hit," I felt a wave of stress. Eager to escape, I reminded him that he had plenty of time for what he was paying me. He thanked me again and asked me to stay just a little while longer–just enough for one more hit, "a tiny bit." Reluctantly, I stayed, but my fear intensified. It was the first time I'd seen someone do a bump, and I can only imagine the look on my face. He laid out the lines and offered me one, but it took me a hundred polite refusals before he grasped how nervous it made me. "I'm sorry if I'm being pushy," he said. "I don't wish this on anyone, but hey, it's good to try it at least–just a little bit. If it's not a good time right now, that's okay, but hey, are you sure?"

Finally, he snorted both lines and warned me it would kick in within fifteen to twenty minutes, tops. I wasn't about to stick around for that, so as soon as he confirmed he could get himself home, I started to get ready to exit the car. Before I did, though–I felt terrible for it–I told him I was going to keep the coins from the cup holder to round off the price. I even considered just taking it; it would be so easy, especially with him so high. But you either make a move like that without thinking, or you don't do it at all–another piece of wisdom I'd picked up from the streets. Three fifty, fourteen total, plus the other thirteen from earlier–it was almost enough. Time to get back to the street!

Next came the only client who treated me like the inflatable doll I'd always dreamed of being! He didn't bargain for the price. He accepted my rate of thirty, plus ten for the room. And wanted everything, full service; he used me freely, and for the first time that night, I smiled and was genuinely turned on, erect and all. We took off our clothes, I was embarrassed about my small breasts, he was looking at me, admiring me, saying that I didn't need breast implants at all, that he liked me as I was, the way I talked, my lighter skin, let me see your asshole, come on. He set me upright in the light and shamelessly examined every inch of my body, slapping me on the booty without asking if he could. Then I let him push me to my knees, and with great pleasure I took that rod in my hands, in my mouth, did whatever I wanted with it, him letting me swallow more and more, deeper and deeper, this man I'd see for free if I didn't need the cash.

"Let's move this to the bed," he said. Would I be able to take it? It was pretty much the same as the last one who had me, and I felt the same pain, so the same thing happened: My dick went soft, but I didn't give up. He wanted to change up positions, things started to click in fits and starts, seeing him so horny made me horny too . . . so I let it happen. In the end, it didn't hurt anymore, though he was the only one who really got off. He came, and I soiled the condom again (ugh, that smell stinking up the room!), but if he noticed, he didn't care. I had a bit of fun nibbling on his head after he took off the condom. When it was time to pay, I only had nine in change from the fifty he gave me, forty-one. Plus the twenty-seven fifty. Phew, now I could kick back and relax. I could make a full one hundred some other time.

06.
TODAY I'LL KNOW LOVE

"And today, Amara Moira knows love: She is going to sleep spooning for the first time with a client who claims to be in love (or maybe, who knows, spend the night tormented by the desire he has for me). 'How much?' The usual—fifty plus transportation, hotel, and meals, nothing more for someone who professes to love me. 'For the whole night?' The whole night. Just you and me, but only this time, okay? (Oh, how I longed to be held like this!) 'Just don't come all sassy and bold . . . in the street, I like you discreet'—look at what he's asking of me, can you believe it? The audacity! The Amara, the one he calls innocent since we first met, is the one he likes best: 'When you're behaved, you're so beautiful.' Fine, then. I can be a nun. Make the most of it. Tomorrow, I will tell you how it went."

Some people are just born suckers, you know what I mean? Seriously. I wrote this two years ago on my way to meet the very first client who wanted to spend the whole night with me. Me, with delusions of love—can you believe it?!

07.
A TRANNY TO DATE

He was in a cold sweat, holding my hand in the middle of the deserted street, just the two of us and a few passing cars. He was the one who grabbed my hand first, eager to show the world that I was his, but he only did it in that empty space where no one could see. Still, I was flattered, and it reminded me of the first time I went to the mall holding hands with my travesti girlfriend, caught between wanting and not wanting to be seen. I was seventeen or eighteen then (and I won't reveal how many years have passed since then to maintain my youthful image). I couldn't help but be amused by my client's unspoken anxiety–a feeling I once shared, now flipped as I became the "person you shouldn't be seen with." Had he wanted to hold my hand ever since we left the bus station? Such boldness seemed to surface only when we reached that strip with the little hotels where the only companions we had were outcasts. Even so, I liked it.

I met him at the bus station with a little peck on the cheek, nothing too intimate, as we made our way to one of those cheap motels for the night. I practiced detachment fiercely, trying to not feel resentful that he'd spent all this money to see me–a hundred for the motel, about thirty-five for his round-trip ticket, plus the occasional taxi–but would only pay me fifty bucks. At least he always came back, at least once a month, and it seemed like he spent all his savings to do so. My friends always warned me not to believe people's sob stories, their excuses for paying us less or sometimes nothing at all. But the truth was, he never tried any of that; I was the one who read between the lines and appreciated his effort. He treated me well, there was also that, and drove me crazy. Plus, the last time I hit the streets, I'd only found three clients and came home cold with a measly eight reais in my pocket. "What you make there, you spend there," another piece of conventional wisdom I had to swallow. Now, at least I could take home the full fifty.

Behind closed doors, he finally kissed me. With the sour breath of someone who'd slept the whole trip, not so great, but little by little I got used to it. He kissed me with the longing of a man who hadn't seen his beloved Amara Moira, or Fernanda, or Melissa, whatever name I'd chosen for him, in a whole month. I kissed him back, craving those kisses too, his kisses, any kisses, as long as they were shared like this. Through these new experiences, I found myself trying to relearn how to kiss, to engage more actively. My old self was gone; I was Amara now, and I felt new concern about kissing like a woman, touching like a woman, hugging like a woman. I wanted to give him all of me as I kissed and hugged him, embracing myself as a woman. Transitioning changes everything; the way you walk, your posture, the way you interact with others, even your tone of voice. I saw these changes more as self-imposed challenges than as true obligations. From there, we started to take off our clothes, each of us fumbling, clumsy. Obviously we were both horny, but I felt like at any moment one of us would do something awkward that would ruin the mood.

To fall asleep on a hairy chest, to be held by manly

arms all night, that was my dream. Before that point, we would still have to have sex; I was hornier than I'd been in ages, so it was what I wanted. The TV was on, just for the background noise and to cast some light on the bed, our stage. Clumsy as only I can be, I got naked, and he did too, kissing me wherever he wanted, tightly wrapping his arms around me ("Construction," he said about where his muscles had come from). Meanwhile, I stood taller than him and had longer arms, but I didn't hug him back and tried not to get in the way of his hugging me because I wanted to feel like I was being protected, his helpless little girl. Sometimes, I'd forget my act and would encircle him with my big arms, closing in on him like a clam, the way I would have done if I were my dead self. The way I never wanted to hug again because it made me feel like a man, and I couldn't feel that way anymore, couldn't let that happen anymore, though he didn't even seem to notice.

I pushed him onto the bed, and he playfully let himself fall, and I got on top of him and took my favorite part of him into my mouth. I was nervous even as I sucked him off, afraid I wouldn't be into it and would have to do it anyway, have to put out, afraid it wouldn't be as good as I'd imagined it, being there for an entire night! But it didn't seem that's how it would go, for the time being. The bed was my territory, and I made it known. I sucked as much as I wanted, his fingers gently tousling my curls, no pressure, and he let me do as I pleased. I started to enjoy it and to do it with more and more gusto, sometimes him holding me back a bit, "or you'll get jizz in your mouth." When he got to that point, I went back to kissing him on the mouth, then I curled up with him so he could hold me, wrap himself around me. And we did that for a long time until he decided to go for what I feared most, to that place that always hurt so much (and I was still naively thinking I just needed more practice).

There wasn't enough lube in the world that could make that sausage go in. I laughed just at the thought of that thing entering my love hole again. This happened every time, but somehow, I always managed to go through with it. It was like a joyless joyride: I completely lost my appetite, goodbye erection, and from then on it was just survival mode, sheer willpower, hoping it would be over soon, pretty please. It hurt putting it in (oh, how it hurt!), and as if that wasn't enough, he still wanted to keep changing positions. And because he'd come all this way (even though he was only giving me a measly fifty reais for the entire night), I felt obliged to accept whatever he wanted. *Rrrrip!* And there went the condom, the first one to break in my entire career: Thank the Goddess for PrEP, that's why I take it, so I don't have to panic at times like this.

We put on a new rubber and got everything back in order, then the impalement ensued, me on the edge of the bed with my legs splayed open, him standing up, going as deep as humanly possible. Thrusting harder and harder, his body all tense, muscles taut, I held on and tried not to scream, tried not to let it show how much I just wanted it to end (it's strange that it was this painful this time, because it had been different before, a tremendous pleasure . . . the anal fissure was only getting worse, I suppose). He came and then collapsed on me, his muscles relaxing, then he hugged me and kissed me. We stayed like that for a while, and I was happy: All I had to do now was sleep and my dreams would come true. But he wanted to talk. Before, he used to just go to sleep.

"Since you won't date me, can you find me a tranny?"

"A tranny?"

"A travesti I can date."

I was speechless. "A tranny." Who would allow anyone, let alone someone who isn't a travesti themselves, to call us something like that? That made my blood boil, even more so with the request that preceded it. I just wanted to enjoy my night on this hairy chest, spooning or whatever, and he dares ask me for a tranny, anyone at all, so he could replace me with her like we're interchangeable? Was that what I'd endured all that pain for? Why did I agree to spend the whole night with him for fifty reais? Oh, what I wouldn't give to be able to tell him to go fuck himself and go home. But at three in the morning, without even having gotten paid yet, there was no way. "Only you, sweetie, would get attached to this quality of man," a friend of mine always says to me, and *grrr*, it was all I could think about lying there in that bed, seething with rage.

"I can't think of anyone I could introduce you to."

And that was that, though this was far from over. I tried to relax, forget about his shadiness, enjoy his hairy chest, his strong arms. We could still pretend we were a couple for a little bit longer. And finally, we slept. The alarm clock rang at 9:30 a.m., we stayed in bed for a bit, no kissing this time (I wasn't in the mood to face his dragon breath after what I'd had to hear), but he woke up horny, with morning wood, and wouldn't leave me alone. I tried to leave, but he wouldn't let me.

For the first time in the three nights I'd been with him, he didn't give a shit about what I wanted: He grabbed my head and pushed it down toward his cock, I had zero desire to suck, I just wanted to go home. He didn't say a word; there was no need to. It was clear he felt entitled to squeeze out one more moment with me—after all, I was still on the clock, right? You know how it goes. I hadn't even received my money yet and had no idea if he would pay extra for this crap, but I let him continue. And there's more: He chose a motel that cost one hundred reais, instead of the one that was just seventy, even though I had said I didn't mind the cheaper option. Was he trying to impress me? Fuck, I'd much rather the extra thirty in my pocket!

I sucked him off without wanting to, my mouth resisting, my body going stiff as a statue. I just wanted to leave. He tried to get in there, but it hurt more than I could handle, still sore from the night before (I would learn, two whole years later, I wasn't fussy or bad at my job). I protested, I protested so much, paralyzed with pain, and he still pushed himself inside of me as if nothing was happening. He only gave in when my complaining finally made his dick soft. Then he took off the condom and came to the edge of the bed to get sucked off, like he was in charge, like he owned my body, and I was so stunned I didn't even know how to say no.

The ease with which he hurt me and kept hurting me, the way he got pleasure out of it, chilled me. Not only because of what it did to me, the situation I was in, but because of how common it is for women, for travestis, to be in that position: to have to go through with intercourse even when pleasure had given way to pain, to violence.

We often imagine rape as a faraway threat, a stranger attacking in the dead of night. In doing so, we overlook how often it occurs day to day, how that violent force can exist in even our most intimate relationships—the relationships we consider romantic.

I gave it my all even though I didn't want to, even

though I was filled with hate. Oblivious to my pain, he blew one of those stupid loads into my mouth just to show that he could, that he was in charge. I ran to spit in the bathroom sink and washed up while I was there, wiped my face. I kept up appearances, I don't even know why, I made small talk while we got dressed. Then I put on a happy face when he gave me the promised amount, fifty reais, and watched in disbelief as he settled up the hundred for the motel in front of me, after having paid me a pittance. More small talk before saying goodbye. Bye bye bye, come back soon. I dashed out as soon as I could, wanting to cry but unable to. I never let myself meet up with him again.

Twenty-nine years of living as a light-skinned cis man, perceived as straight despite being bi, and raised middle class. When I transitioned and started to be seen as a travesti, it was then that I experienced sexual violence for the first time. I had always felt powerful, taught to stand up to anyone, yet I couldn't stop this client from forcing me to continue despite all the pain. I felt not just physical pain, but also the psychic pain of being unable to say no. My visible suffering wasn't enough to make him stop; maybe he even got some twisted thrill from knowing his dick could hurt someone who fucks for a living.

08.
A DIFFERENT KIND OF SIXTY-NINE

It was already a tough night; the mosquitos wouldn't leave us alone, and it was hot, hot, hot. Then a man in his forties rode up on a motorcycle, looking a bit rough around the edges. Without an introduction, he asked, "You want to be my girlfriend?" Politely, I said, "I can't do that, that's not how this works. But I could turn you a nice trick." He launched into his life story. "I have two kids, my wife cheated on me while I was out breaking my back to support us. I almost killed the bitch. Now I live alone with my brother. I can pay your bills and still allow you to keep working here." What a luxury. He winked at me conspiratorially, but I wasn't impressed. "Oh, honey, I appreciate the offer, but we hardly know each other. There's no love here."

"Are you new here? How much to spend a night with me at my place?"

"One hundred." I stood firm on my price, the goal for the night all in one go, and to my surprise, he accepted. I could hardly believe I was about to head home with the money I needed so easily. Yet part of me was scared shitless that I might actually be falling for a trick–he was so sweet, constantly reassuring me, "Come on . . . I'm respectful, you can trust me. There's no risk." I gave him my number, and we agreed he'd call me at 10 p.m., so we could leave around 11 p.m. Little did I know, the night had something even better in store—I wouldn't need to answer the phone or venture outside the neighborhood!

After two hours of battling the heat and mosquitoes, all I'd gotten was this zaddy on the motorcycle. Once he left and the initial excitement faded, I felt a twinge of fear about going away with an older man to sleep God knows where. With no clients for hours, I started to think I'd settle for thirty out of pocket and head home, feeling sad and disappointed. Just then, a burly guy in his fifties with a beer belly approached, asking for my tricks. He didn't even negotiate, accepting the price of forty right off the bat so we could get started. I was relieved—forty would cover the room and expenses (R$10 for the room, R$30 for the night's expenses), plus I could keep the hundred from Mr. "Want to be My Girlfriend?" if I chose to go with him. But with this guy, forty was just the beginning. Once we reached the room, he whipped out a fifty and said, "Don't worry about change. I just want you—come here." He kept pleading, "I need you; can you take care of me," so childish it was annoying. "Uh-huh, of course I can," I replied. "I love a needy man; I'll take care of you real nice."

He stripped down and asked if he could take a shower, but the room didn't have one, let alone soap. What did he expect for ten reais an hour? He didn't look dirty, so I decided to just get it over with and get back out there. But as soon I went down on him, I had to spit out sand—sand, of all things! Had he been playing in a sandbox before coming to see me? I had to stop. "Let's wash up a bit in the sink, at least you should." He obliged without a hint of shame.

At this point, he started asking about a credit card machine. "I wonder if they have one here. If they do, I can give you another fifty so you can relax and take your time—however long it takes. I don't have any cash left, see? Otherwise, I'd pay extra." He then proceeded to show me the contents of his wallet, item by item. I honestly wasn't sure if the hotel had a machine; I was still new to this and figured they might not. I mentioned there was one at the hotel down the street, where I preferred to meet clients since they definitely had a shower—and with any luck, even soap. "We'll figure it out later then. Come here, I want to enjoy you a little more; I really need you right now." He was surprised when I kissed him. "Oh, that feels nice," he said, but he wouldn't let me put my tongue in his mouth, only using the tip of his own when he leaned in for what he called a kiss. His breath was overpowering, but the promise of fifty bucks, and maybe more, helped me ignore it. I thought it was odd, but only because I couldn't have guessed what was coming later; otherwise, I would have saved that word, *odd*, for a different moment.

The struggle soon began. I worked on his flaccidness, but nothing could get him hard. And yet he wouldn't stop moaning, "So nice," he said. As I worked with my tongue, lips, hand, trying every tool in my toolbox—which had many—his softness started to affect me. Usually, it's the other person's hardness that gets me hard too. Then he asked, maybe realizing I wasn't making progress, to put my finger in his cornhole, in his bum. I was only worried I might get dirty. Remember, soap wasn't exactly easy to come by around these parts. But I was desperate. "So be it," I thought. "Time to get dirty." I fondled him around the rim, gently, while working his limp dick from the base with my mouth and hand, but it still didn't respond. I lightly pushed the tip of my finger into his asshole. Jesus Christ, why did I do that? Now he wanted me to go deeper. I suggested a condom and lube so I could put it in real good. I didn't have the nerve to look, much less smell, to check on my brave little finger!

I just put my two fingers in a condom to see if he could take it (if I'd known better, I would have started with my whole fist). I started prodding his asshole, lightly at first, then I saw how easily it went in and how much he liked it, so I went deeper, then deeper, as far as I could go, merciless and also afraid my nails might tear the condom! His reaction was always the same, more moaning, "That feels so nice," "Oh yeah," stuff like that. Still, he was not hard, but nonetheless seemed to be enjoying it . . . We stayed there for half an hour, just me prodding him, until he suggested we go to that other room, where there was a shower and he could get more money: "Another fifty, is that all right? Or maybe even a hundred, so you can relax, then there's no hurry, right?" I left him waiting in the room while I went to return the key, then we took his car one block over to the other place.

A new room, another ten bucks for the hour. The first thing he did was take a good shower: Now there was a shower and, more than that, an old piece of soap. I stood there at the door watching him wash up, admiring this hairy, beer-bellied man. He called me in, I joined him but tried not to get my hair wet (there was only a small towel for him, nothing left for me). We stayed there making out until I had enough. "We're done! We've wasted enough water!" He asked if he should "clear the pipes," and I encouraged it. While I probed in his hole earlier, I thought I would find a gaping emptiness, but it wasn't empty at all. He strained for a bit, finished his number two, then went back to the shower to touch up his cleaning. I was already lying in bed, drying with the fan.

He had already offered me fifty reais before we went into the room, but then out of nowhere he said, "Oh no, a hundred is fine," adding, "You know what? Better make it a hundred and fifty," without me saying a word. He even insisted on covering an extra fifteen for the 10 percent he assumed would go to the house. All this charged to his card, on top of the fifty he'd already paid in cash for the other room. All he wanted to know was if I was going to make it real nice for him and take my time, if I'd care for him the way he needed me to. I assured him I would, saying, "I'm having the best time here with you!" Only later did I realize why he was offering me all this money. I caught myself feeling a little tempted by him, almost forced into doing things I still can't decide whether to write about or take to my grave.

He came to bed, asked to sixty-nine, and off we went. Neither of our dicks got hard, a real battle of limp with limp, when suddenly, I felt him sniffing around other parts. Two seconds and he was in my bumhole, right in my ass, the new playground he found for his tongue. I abandoned the sixty-nine, otherwise I'd have to contort myself to pull it off. He went in, licked around it, played with everything, passionately using his tongue to explore every pore in my asshole, and me finding it all very amusing, seeing that old bore start to come to life. Then came the bullshit. "How about a different kind of sixty-nine?" Different how? "Ah . . . you mean . . . back there!" And he licked wherever he wanted without even asking anymore, licking a precursor to "I can give you another fifty." Jesus Christ, what a proposal! But for fifty more, and already feeling indebted to him, swimming in all his dough, I found myself nibbling on it a bit, teasing here and there. He went, "Wow, my Goddess, that's wonderful . . . Leave this to me."

I suggested using the dildo I kept in my bag, and he liked the idea. So I went to grab my toy. I got back and he was very comfortably lying on the bed, naked and hairy, with a pillow under his butt to lift it up a bit. I put a condom on the dildo and got on top of him. This time it went in without any lube and that was when I realized that if I had put my whole fist in instead of just two fingers, he would have liked it much more. We spent almost half an hour just going in and out, in and out, him asking me the entire time, "Are you giving it to me, babe? Are you doing me good? Destroying my ass? Ass raping me?" I said "Yes" and repeated whatever bullshit he said to me, without the same level of passion. I was getting more and more tired of the whole thing. I tried a few variations to shake things up, like calling him a little bitch, treating him like a femme, but he didn't seem too into it, so I went back to the rough stuff he liked, afraid I'd lose the client. *Bam! Bam! Bam!* "Will the romance ever end," I thought to myself.

The hotel manager knocked on the bedroom door, gently hurrying us along. He quickly replied, "I can give you another fifty later, then we can stay longer, right?" Since the minimum charge on a credit card was eighty, I suggested he put that amount on the card, and I'd give him the change in cash. My eyes sparkled with hope that he'd say "No need."

"Oh, no need," he said. "Just buy me a beer from the food truck across the street when we're done, and we'll be even." I informed the manager that we'd be staying a bit longer, and she nodded in agreement before we settled back into our time together.

But it was time to be direct: it was time for him to cum for me, and he nodded yes, he'd like to cum with me sitting on his face, right on his mouth. A setup, I was shocked when I felt him firmly pushing my butt crack open so he could thrust his tongue deeper and deeper, digging even . . . as much as he lacked a hard cock, he had a good tongue, and he seemed delighted to explore all the nooks and crannies inside my hole. My impression was that he wanted to try even my most intimate flavors, if that makes sense; I really tried to figure out if that's what he was after. The douche had worked this time around, though, and he could barely taste anything. At any rate, two minutes of that and for the first time, his dick came up to a semi, just enough for him to be able to maybe cum. I continued jerking him off while he penetrated me with his tongue and muttered moans, almost screaming, until finally milk started to freely flow out of his member. I held on for a bit longer, extracting every last drop. Phew, done at last. We quickly cleaned up and settled the bill before heading out for that well-deserved beer. He was being all affectionate, like he was my boyfriend. "I'll come back soon, okay?" he said, Goddess willing! I paid for the beer, but that was fine; I was treating myself, celebrating that night's glimpse of wealth.

09.
THINGS SAID BETWEEN TRAVESTIS

"Fuck, honey! That man, can you believe he asked me to take a dump on his dick? I mean, I'm glad it was his cock and not his mouth, because you *know* some freak might want that. Still, three hours wasted douching only for a motherfucker like that to show up. And you know the second I smear the condom, after they'd been poking in there for hours and hours, they will throw a fit, make a scene, 'That's disgusting, fuck this, fuck you!' But when *they* do that it's perfectly normal, they'll still ask for a rim job and everything, my tongue with no condom on their hairy balls, their hot milk in my mouth, 'Trust me, I'm married, a blood donor.' Uh huh, sure. And here I was thinking they'd fuck my brains out, put their mouth straight on my asshole as soon as we got to the room–but I blinked, and the pussy was on my dick. Fuck!"

10.
THE OGS

The other day, I logged into a chatroom to promote my blog. I chose the nickname "Travesti Escritora" and did the same song and dance for everyone, the same thing I have to do when people come and ask me, "You're a writer of what?!" The song and dance goes like this: "I love turning a naughty little trick and then writing all about it on my blog," I say, and then I share a hand-picked excerpt, plus the link to my blog, people chomping at the bit to read the latest hot filthy goss. Sometimes, people get excited and ask me, "Is there a phone number? And a photo? How big? What do you do?" The same old story professional travestis know all too well. Some have wanted me to write something right there, maybe so they could finish themselves off and leave me hanging (they underestimate my intelligence, poor things). All I say is I can't make stuff up, I'm only good at retelling my experiences, you'd have to pay to find out what I'm like, you up for it? And usually, nothing. This is new to me, attracting clients through the promise of a story later, as my earlier clients couldn't have dreamed their stories might make their way onto the internet (and maybe even into a book, imagine. Maybe one of them will find out sooner or later and come after me . . . ideas for my next book, who knows!).

The most interesting person in this particular chatroom was the one who said he would give me a hundred and sixty reais for the traditional full service, easy—that is, if I spanked him with Havaianas flip-flops afterward. I frantically scoured the house for a pair of Havaianas, and I got back to him, hesitant: "Look, I'll even spank you for free (imagine how funny, a grown man taking a flip-flop spanking from *moi*, cute little marks on his skin, my meek command, "Oh, don't you dare make a sound!"). But I only have Ipanema flip-flops! Will that do?" He asked for a photo of the flip-flops, I sent him one, and he left the chat. You get what you pay for, I guess. I'd bought the cheaper Ipanema sandals thinking flip-flops were all the same and ended up losing money. Mierda.

11.
ON THE HOOD
OF THE CAR

I hate when I have to go home with less money than what I started with, since I have to pay out of pocket to go to work. There's a point in the night when despair sets in; I'm already plotting what I can do to break even before the night ends. I don't have the stamina, much less the mental fortitude, to spend hours out here waiting for something to happen. It was already 9 p.m. when I got there (generally, I felt more comfortable on the streets at night, enveloped by darkness, and it had been raining before), and I planned to stop at around 11 p.m. (wishful thinking) and take the last bus home . . . of course it went nothing like that. Nine p.m., nothing, ten p.m., nothing, ten thirty p.m., and rien de rien (nothing at all). Would this finally be the day I returned home utterly empty-handed? The chill after the rain was starting to give me shivers when finally, finally, a freak came up to me looking for a good time. Thirty bucks, in the parking lot. I climbed into his car, everything was fine, but as soon as I looked at him, he hit me with the usual "Can't you do it for twenty?" You give them an inch, let them open their mouths, and that's what you get. Well, better twenty in my pocket than in his; you already know I hated to lose what little had come my way, so you can imagine what I said. Let me give you a taste of our dialogue, so you can see just what he was like:

"What do you do, babe?"

"Everything, but I'm better as a bottom."

"I'm the top here, you can leave that to me. Are you a good kisser?"

"This is how I kiss," then I kissed his hot little mouth.

"That's hot. And have you already given up that ass today, you dirty ho?"

"You're my first, I only work from time to time... I'm tight as a duck's ass, you'll see."

"Right, I bet it's gaping by now! And if I want to suck it?"

"Sounds great, I love a good tongue."

I said it just like that, straight up, no holds barred, and also said he'd spend the night blissed out of his mind. In the parking lot, cash already in my pocket, we kissed and kissed, his hand on my cock over my panties, heavy petting, and here and there something a little gentler. I was actually enjoying it, I'll admit. Then he pushed back the driver's seat, unzipped his pants, and I got to work, and all the while he praised my performance. Before I had gotten into his car, while we were negotiating the price, I gave his junk a naughty little squeeze to size it up, at which point he said, "It's small," and it really did seem small, to my relief. Oh, how looks and feels can deceive: He had a monstrous anaconda, and as it grew in my mouth, I started to panic. "Do you like getting hit in the face, puta?" he asked. I said "Only affectionately," but he was already coming at me with an open palm; fuck what I like. I didn't like that, but he didn't care, and he slapped me a few more times.

We got out of the car and stepped into the bushes. Now that our business in the front was done, he wanted to party in the back, but I knew—me, the unlucky narrator of this story, who at that point still had a tight ass–that this would be no party. Oh, how it would hurt, how unimaginable the pain! He splayed my legs on the hood of the car and wagged his tongue in my freshly douched hole while I held onto the hood with all my might so I wouldn't slide down. He completely missed my reactions, thinking I was just being fussy, while I gritted my teeth. We couldn't stay like that, and look, I'm not even talking about the impalement that was yet to come. I told him, "That's enough, let me go on all fours so it's good for everyone."

But it wasn't good. It hurt like hell; he slapped my butt cheeks, and that hurt, too, and that was what I got for the night. It took forever for him to finally get in. By then, any sign of a boner I had was long gone, but I kept focused and tried not to stall things so it would be over soon. The pain was so overpowering I went numb at one point, and I didn't feel when he finished. He said he was crazy about me, made a point of getting my phone number, giving me a kiss, "But this is between us, promise? My wife . . . I can't mess that up." When he left, I took a deep breath, quickly cleaned my love hole (I had toilet paper in my bag, otherwise I'd have to wipe myself with my panties), and got on with my life.

12.
MY PORN DEBUT

"You want to do it?"

"Oh, I don't know . . . and what if people see it, Jesus!"

"Nah, no need to worry about that, it's for a European audience, not a chance."

"But would we get paid for this?"

"Five hundred for you because you're a man. Travestis get more, eight hundred."

"And what would we have to do?"

"We'd have sex, of course, the same way we do all the time, real nice and naughty."

That was how my girlfriend at the time, a travesti, asked me to be in a movie with her. She was in very high demand for pornos, having just started her transition—she was still wearing a wig and didn't even have little hormone breasts yet, but she had an impressive nine-inch knocker, hung like a horse, and at the same time, incredibly feminine, truly a beautiful woman. At around twenty years old, I was a dumb boy, trying to live vicariously through her transition, to experience through her what I wouldn't dare imagine for myself. We would spend a whole afternoon at a farm on the outskirts of São Paulo, several films being shot together, transportation and food covered: We just had to fuck, and that was it. And it was 2005, another era; we couldn't imagine yet what the internet would become, so I believed her when she said the movie would only be available in Europe.

We douched up well ("There can't be any fudge when it's time, okay? Keep going until the water comes out clear") and went to the bedroom. A production assistant gave me half a Viagra as a boost because I was nervous—everyone was very understanding, no pressure. But it was still a very stressful day. The camera made me uncomfortable, and I already had a complicated relationship with my dick, so I couldn't get hard. They left us alone in the room, just the camera and the two of us. Still, I couldn't get hard. Another Viagra, the camera rolling, and I played the bottom in the meantime (no condom, that's what it's like for partners), but I couldn't do the other part. Finally, they got tired of waiting and brought in a strange contraption, a ketchup bottle full of a shampoo-based paste that looked like cum. I got my dick as hard as I could, they squeezed the bottle, and wham! It looked like I had cum.

I usually did it easily and out of pleasure because it's my vice. "Doing it for the vice" means enjoying it, doing it for the hell of it, doing it for free in travesti lingo, known as bajubá. I'm up for any adventure, but doing it in front of the camera, as it eyed me, followed my every move, had me shaking with fear. The funny thing was that in over a month of dating my girlfriend, that shoot was the only time I had sex with her without whimpering in pain, the only time I felt real pleasure feasting on her dick. I got the cash, but the crew obviously never called me again. I wasn't traumatized or anything, but I did carry around this lingering fear that someone would find the damn movie someday; a fear I carried until the beginning of this year, when I got tired of keeping it a secret and went shouting this story from the rooftops—how terribly I performed, how hard it is to find the tape online, and how even if someone found it, I'd doubt they'd recognize me.

But I remember very well what my girlfriend said about it, and these days, when I hear people who aren't in the industry proposing to ban this genre of film (or end sex work), I think: "Hey sweetie, why don't you go and propose the end of your own profession?" It was eight hundred reais per movie at the time, and she was doing several per week: Now, I ask you how many tricks (on average about seventy reais each) would she have had to turn to make that kind of money? In one afternoon, making two or three films, she'd earn the equivalent of about thirty tricks, and only having sex with people she knew, without the risk of violence, with people she trusted and who treated her well.

She only found clients through the internet, as she was afraid of going out on the streets; she'd recently arrived in São Paulo from a smaller town in the northeast and had to send money home to help her mother. Those movies were an absolute godsend in her life. And on some level, she did it for the vice, like me, but way more, because no camera was going to inhibit all her energy, her endless desire to fuck. She had no problem surrendering herself completely to whatever scene—she wore the team's jersey, so to speak, she did it for pleasure and enjoyed it.

Years later, when I threw myself into making homemade content for adult platforms (especially content for fetishists), she was my greatest inspiration. But I'll save that for another book.

13.
ON TOP AND LIKING IT

An incredible thing sex work has done for me–or to me, that is: Bodies I'd never allow myself to get intimate with now lie naked next to me, rub against me, as we experience the greatest pleasure. It takes minimal effort on my part, I just throw myself into it, and the pleasure comes on its own, pushing against whatever conditioning I'd received to only be interested in certain bodies that fall within beauty standards (of course, this also depends on the cooperation of clients, the way they treat me, that they come with good-smelling, musky dicks that become somewhat easily erect, and so on).

I just needed enough money to cover the basics so I could finally go home and sleep after more than three hours braving the cold streets. Then a fancy car pulled up, and the driver rolled down the window. "How much?" he asked. "Forty, plus the room." "Get in." Just like that–no haggling, no disrespecting my work. The motel I suggested was full, so I proposed the drive-in instead. It was my first time venturing beyond this familiar territory, the safe haven where I knew that if one of us screamed, someone would hear and hopefully come running. I charged thirty reais for three hours at the drive-in, which included a bed and a bathroom. I expected him to complain, but he didn't say a word; not a peep! We entered.

I was already sore from the client I'd seen a few hours earlier, so I was nervous about how this would go. We hadn't made any plans for what we'd do in bed, I had no idea what to expect. He swept me off my feet with a heartfelt "You're so beautiful!" I leaped into his arms, another bear with a beer belly, though a touch more effeminate. His beard grazed my face, and his breath suggested he'd knocked back a few drinks. Kiss, kiss, kiss, I can't even count how many, as we rolled around in bed, lost in the moment. For a minute, I thought that was all we were there to do. I asked him if he wanted me to suck him, and he shut me up with even more kisses before I could finish my sentence. The two of us fully naked, our cocks erect and ready to go, and I kept noticing him meandering by my ass, poking around my hole, as if he'd end up in there by chance.

At one point, I got out of bed to try to go down on him—otherwise, we'd have spent the whole night like that, which was nice and all, but he wasn't my boyfriend. All it took was my hard cock passing close to his mouth and he shamelessly took a little nibble. A weird experience; I found it pleasurable to be touched like that, I won't deny it, with that intense intimacy and desire helping me get free in my body. "You are so beautiful," he said again, his mouth full, drooling over me, the compliment weakening my knees. Soon, it was my turn to go for it, and I stayed down there for a long time, then longer, until he asked to sixty-nine (unthinkable for me a year ago, but look at me now). I was so turned on that my cock ached because we'd been rubbing against each other for a while and the hormones made it a bit sensitive (imagine estrogen with a testosterone blocker . . . I was going crazy).

We went back to kissing, and this time, instead of coming for my ass, he wanted me to go for his, even trying to get me to "accidentally" slip my cock into his little hole, and I noticed he kept avoiding putting on the condom. At some point, I stopped everything and said: "Time to wrap the present, yours or mine?" Mine then, okay. "You're so beautiful," he repeats, as I blush all over. Problem is, condoms can be like this: As I put one on, I went soft, and the hormones didn't help. But we still played a bit. I got behind him with my big hook, trying to catch worms, to borrow from the poet Gregório de Matos. I wasn't as hard as before, his asshole was so tight, it took me so long to get inside, my erection dying out. He, sweetly, without complaining, got ready for his turn to try; he was still hard, and I was still sore. I struggled, I struggled hard until he got his release, until he was overcome with pleasure, flooding the condom!

After that, he became another person. No more hugs, affection, nothing of the sort. He got ready in a flash, as did I, following his pace; once he was ready, he took a fat wad of bills out of his wallet, and instead of the forty we'd agreed on, he gave me seventy. With what I'd made earlier, that was almost my goal for the day, not including the thirty for the drive-in. But all the intimacy was gone, and I no longer recognized the person who'd made me so horny, who'd had me on all fours feeling so loved. I'd made the mistake of bringing my neediness to work again. He brought me back to the spot where he'd picked me up, gave me a little peck goodbye, and that's how my night ended.

14.
FREEBIE

Remember the guy on the motorcycle? He showed up drooling with lust. I gently rubbed his package and felt it grow as his jeans tightened. Twenty for a blowjob in the bushes, that's the price, I told him. His eyes twinkled playfully. I walked toward the spot we'd agreed on, and he followed on his motorcycle. We were still making our way there when he called out to me with the cursed, predictable ask, "How about fifteen?" At this point, I was about to tell the little shit to go to hell, but instead I leaned closer to him, fondled him a little more, my hands on the curves of his groin, his junk. "Are you sure you can't do twenty? You're disrespecting my work, love." In that moment, I felt his jeans getting wet and I was taken aback, not yet understanding what had happened; he was soaked and getting my fingers sticky. He had a look on his face like that of a naughty little boy. Then he revved up his motorcycle and took off without so much as a word. I had made the bastard cum for free; I couldn't believe it! I'd been told to be careful, to use my powers sparingly. For him to offer so little, then try to whittle it down more, and ultimately leave me hanging? And people want to know why I use such vile language to talk about my clients– those bastards!

15.
SHITTY MEN OUTDO THEMSELVES

Motorcycles and cars passed by us all night, some very slowly so the drivers could check us out, while others pretended not to see us. It's hard to say which was worse—probably the broke men who tried to get a taste for free. Prize goes to the man who had the nerve to ask me if I'd go out with him for ten bucks. As his car disappeared around the corner, I fantasized about flat tires and car crashes. Where are our superpowers when we need them?

16.
TODAY I DIDN'T MAKE A MESS

With a headache, runny nose, sneezing, zero patience for assholes, and it being so cold outside . . . I should have stayed home for the day, but what did I do instead? I douched, really well, too, forty minutes of abdominal pain from all the water I'd forced into my ass. I'd never felt so intensely, intestinally clean! I was happier than usual going out into the street, feeling lighter with the certainty that there'd be no mess today; I could already picture all the money I would make.

There, I waited standing at the corner–big mistake. I tried changing places, went to the other side of the street, put on more lipstick, fixed my clothes, and still not a single bite. Some asshole finally arrived, wanting full service in the parking lot for twenty–something I might have done last week, but tonight I didn't feel like doing that after all my meticulous douching (it's a thorny question: The bigger the cock, the bigger the damage, which might have forced me to close up shop for the night for a mere twenty bucks, you understand?). He promised the same thing they all promise, to go get a fiver from his friends. "I'll be right back."

I should have taken his money, because while he was gone, that other loser who'd paid me twenty last week for the whole deal in the parking lot showed up: He'd been calling me all week, asking to meet up, saying he would come see me, and what did he do? He came, but with only nine reais in his pocket, the asshole. He was even a stingy old miser about the loose coins on the dashboard. No shame whatsoever–"Give me a kiss, I miss you, let's have a good time, there's just one problem." The same bullshit, my God I was pissed, hell no, fuck off! "But come on, not even a handjob for nine bucks?" I relented. Let's go then, let's get this over with and move on; the aim was to get to thirty bucks as soon as possible without even using my recently douched cornhole.

We headed to the parking lot as I warmed him up. When we arrived, he started asking for unreasonable stuff, a little kiss here and there, then "Will you take off your clothes, will you let me touch it, will you wet just the tip with your tongue, come on, just a little lick? I'm almost there." I was so annoyed, and he just shrugged me off, saying, "Don't be like that"–the bastard. He wanted to get out of the car so we could finish outside. Seriously, it shouldn't have lasted more than ten minutes for what he paid me–ten minutes if I'm being generous–but it ended up being at least thirty minutes of faffing about. I tried to hurry things along, more and more disgusted with the idiots that keep showing up, until I felt the hot squirt run through my fingers in the darkness of the parking lot– the two of us leaning against the hood, the car moving if we applied pressure because apparently the handbrake "wasn't all that."

I swore I would never let this idiot touch me again for less than thirty bucks. And not because of the price, but because I was exhausted from his abuse, him calling me a slut, asking how many guys I'd fucked that day, treating me like shit, slapping me, then wanting to suck my dick, my ass, and trying to kiss me after, me avoiding his mouth like the plague. Who did he think I was? But finally, we finished, I got my nine bucks, and after that, I spent hours doing nothing. All the other girls meanwhile making bank, me feeling terrible that the only guys who talked to me wanted it for free or worse; sometimes, they even ask me how much I'd pay to go out with them. So much bullshit, such clowns. Then people have the nerve to say travestis are violent. We rob one of these fuckers and everyone's like, "Oh my God, why would they do that?" Seriously?

I just wanted to go home knowing I made more than I'd spent, you know? And I could not get there fast enough. I only needed twenty-one more, and then I'd be happy to call it a night. I waited and waited and waited until someone came to my rescue: the man who'd allow me to go sleep in peace (they always show, just have faith, my colleagues say). Straight away he asked what I was, a male or female.

"Travesti."

"I know, but very feminine?"

"Very."

Sometimes I felt like I was rehearsing an absurdist play. We agreed on prices chaotically, so we set off without even being clear on whether he wanted oral or the whole deal. I needed to see the money, thirty bucks, which he paid in advance. His big cock was already hard as soon as he'd stopped the car; he took off his clothes so they wouldn't get dirty. I took my mouth down to where it would be working, but then, something I'd never heard: He grabbed me with his arms and said, "Wait a minute, slow down, what about the condom?"

He made me question what I'd been doing there; all the education I could be pushing on these bastards, the risks I'd been taking for free because I wanted to enjoy my work. I thought they wouldn't go out with me if I insisted on a condom for oral. Sucking dick, the thing I like the most, so I was happy to do it without protection—then this one comes along, demanding it before we play; and after I had just gotten a talking-to from our travesti godmother, the closest thing many of us had to a mentor, for taking these kinds of risks. "It's hard to get AIDS from oral, but syphilis is easy-peasy," she said, a proverbial slap on the wrist.

We put on the rubber, the condom, and started over, him now going for my dick and massaging it so aggressively I couldn't help but feel pleasure. "Doesn't it get hard?" Where did these guys learn to fuck? For Goddess's sake. "Look, honey, it's not like that, sometimes it gets hard, but before it does, I have to be horny, and that's not happening." I was subtler than that. He obviously didn't pick up on it. Then he started to complain that I wouldn't be able to fuck him like this (ah, so that's what he was expecting? Good to know!). I thought it was weird that his giant cock was right there and yet he didn't want my mouth or hand or anything anywhere near it; turns out he just wanted my dick to get hard so he could ride it! I keep thinking I'm an open-minded person, but in times like these, I see that maybe I'm not as down as I imagine—after all, what's so wrong with a man with a big dick wanting a ride?

Since I couldn't give him what he wanted, he asked me to fondle his asshole. I grabbed another condom, the second one of the night, wrapped two fingers and got started, my disgust evident on my face (I tried to look elsewhere to shield myself from the smell). He asked me to stick my fingers in, and there they went, no lube needed, both fingers at the same time, while he frantically masturbated until he climaxed. After that, the usual: He barely looked me in the eye, he didn't say another word to me, and I left as quickly as possible, so I didn't have to deal with his embarrassment. But, in the end, I was thrilled; at least I would go home with a few bucks.

17.
RADICALTRAVESTIS

"I'm not well, I'm stressed. Better leave before clients start showing up. If I see another bottom, I might end up choking him to death."

"Then choke him, girl! And charge him five hundred bucks for it. Tell him, 'And you're not allowed to cum!'"

18.
MEN WILL BE MEN

I don't know if it's because I've been writing about my work and thus reflecting on past experiences, or if it's because my work really is that violent and I'm only realizing it now–but with every client, my experience on the streets becomes more reminiscent of abuse, harassment, rape. Whether the condom breaks and the client keeps going anyway (I often wonder if they somehow make it break on purpose); whether they try to stick it in without a condom or ask to pay to raw-dog me (the stories I've heard of men who take it off without the travesti noticing, or of men who put a gun to travestis' heads to force them to fuck without protection); this whole time, all this pressure for me to do whatever clients tell me to, all the verbal violence, all the lies and lines about their wives ("I'm married, I can't fuck around")–and then my anal fissure as the cherry on top. All of these things have radically transformed my thinking on prostitution.

If in the beginning there was genuine pleasure, with my desire to learn about my body and to be loved–and those two things, those interests and wants, are still present, strong and steady within me–now what I feel most is pain. And when I go back to my other world, to my life at the university, a world of supposedly smarter, better people, I find the same crap, just more subtle. Jokes that normalize rape, men proudly parading their mistresses, men having fun and treating all women as potential prey, as objects, declaring who's hot and who's not, women's voices silenced and stigmatized. "If you don't know how to behave in a man's world, shut up and listen." The bird they flip to the experiences of so many women on campus, single mothers especially.

It's hard to deal with all of this without drawing a very direct connection between masculinity and rape—as much as I agree with my friend who said that that connection erases how women and travestis are also part of the same sexist system, that none of us are immune from reproducing the same dynamics that uphold the patriarchy. Maybe that's why I've been trying to radically transform myself as a person, because the man I used to be couldn't be trusted. He/I didn't know it, and now I see he didn't really want to learn either.

19.
SOMETIMES SHIT HAPPENS

I still hadn't bought a bidet to help me douche, the easiest way to do it, so I ended up using one of those pharmacy kits that are supposedly made for it, though I could never make them work as well. I fill the rubber bulb with water, fit the tube onto the bulb, put it in my ass (which always hurts, either because I didn't use enough lube or because of the damn fissure), and I squeeze. After doing this three times, enough for the water to fill my intestine, the liquid starts to weigh me down; three times and I can't take it anymore, I run to the toilet to let it all out before it gets even messier.

I repeat these steps about ten times before the water runs clear as if it hadn't come from my ass (until then, the filth is brutal, the smell is foul, good lord!). But why do this? Well, so as to not soil the condom or client, so he can poke, prod, shove his cock deep into my hole, the end of my excretory system, without getting acquainted with my most intimate smells or seeing my creaminess when he takes out his wiener. It also helps the client feel more comfortable sucking my ass, though it seems many don't seem to worry one bit about this: You can't even imagine how many men go straight to it without even bothering to ask about hygiene–and the gusto with which they do it, twisting their whole bodies so their tongue can dig as deep as possible. It makes me wonder if they'd get frustrated when they can't taste anything at all or sniff a faint aroma to remember me by. To each their own, right?

The douche doesn't always work though, whether because my bowels are in constant motion or because I put my body to work all day, things going in and out, prompting my intestines to move faster than normal. One thing is for certain: Even the best-done douche is overcome eventually. The funny thing is that most of the bottoms I meet will make a mess and not say a word, but when it happens to one of us, they make a scene. For example, as one piece-of-shit regular told my friend after an episode like this: "Wow, you're a pig in a pigsty, aren't you, I can't go out with you anymore!" Because shit came out of her little shitter, imagine that. And the worst part is, this never happens with clients who are into it. The scat lovers only show up when you've put a lot of effort into douching. Murphy's Law.

Then self-righteous people come and criticize me for naming the trash, trash; the daddies, daddies. No one ever asks a travesti beforehand if she's douched: They treat it like it's an obligation, a moral duty, and fuck it if douching destroys our guts, if it damages our rectums over time, if we spend an hour using liters of treated water in times of drought. They want to eat ass like it's any hole, and not the one that it is; these are the same men who get angry when I use a condom for blowjobs, because *they* don't accept that, and I don't accept risking STDs for twenty reais, sometimes less. And even if it were more, the risk still wouldn't be worth it, shouldn't be worth it. That's why I'm proud to have soiled nearly everyone who's fucked me so far—so they remember what trash they are. I'd love to see them complain!

20.
HATE BITE

You might think I'm overreacting, I bet, but oh well—here we go. After I hit a crisis point with that merciless string of bastards, I finally worked up the nerve to get back in the saddle. The result was as expected: catastrophic. I like to work at night, I don't like the sun on my face, so by the time I hit the streets, it was past 8 p.m., already dark, a little chilly. Nearly no one was out there, everywhere was empty because of Carnaval and the threat of rain. Cars passed by without as much as a glance in my direction, most of them pretending I didn't exist, picking up speed whenever I dare notice them. I don't know what's worse, the cars that ignore me or the ones that stop just to make fun of me, pretending to be interested—and yesterday they were all trying to test my patience. It's bad when they ignore me, but it's worse or at least just as bad when they stop.

One showed up and complimented me on how affectionate I was, but he hated that I wouldn't go on top, let alone enjoy it (come on, the hormones make it hard!). Finally, he asked if I would at least snort a little powder with him, if I would score us some—me of all people, the purest of the bunch. He looked disgusting, sweaty, sitting a little sullen. "Okay then, I'll just go for a little ride and come back later." Sometimes, I think it would be best if we worked like taxi drivers, where you take the first in line; no matter what you're looking for, a ride is a ride. The street feeds a terrible competitiveness amongst us, all of us thinking a customer didn't come for us because somebody else had a better body, straighter hair, a more impressive ass, who knows, breasts that defy the laws of gravity. Plenty to make us want to get under the knife, schedule an injection, rush to get implants, spend thousands on salons, aestheticians, clothes, makeup.

Yesterday alone, I was told to straighten my hair, wear better clothes, and where's your makeup, bitch? But if I did all that, Jesus, how long would it take me working my ass off to make back all that dough? It's hard enough as it is; imagine the pressure of making little to no cash on top of all those expenses. Not to mention it's hard to get excited to dress up for these bastards and shitheads who don't give a fuck. They have no idea if I've put on eyeliner or mascara or anything at all: If they want it, they'll take it, and that's that. Where are the sweet men from the beginning who used to treat me like a doll, who barely asked me to lift a finger? Was it beginner's luck, or was I just naïve back then, and not realizing in my excitement that they were just as bad?

Yesterday was one of those particularly shitty, hopeless days. An old man stopped in his old clunker, wearing nothing but boxer shorts, gray hairs on his arm, ugly as sin, and even nastier manners. He wanted full service; we could do it for forty plus the cost of the room, but he just made a face until he reached out, grabbed my head, and pulled it toward his face like he wanted a kiss . . . and I let him, even though his breath smelled awful, even from a distance. Yeah, it seemed like he wanted a kiss, but what did he do instead? He bit my cheek, it hurt, it even left a mark! "Do you like love bites? I want to bite you all over!"

"Not like that," I said, sulking. "Easy, please." I wanted to curse the bastard, punch him in the teeth, but I made like I wasn't deeply offended. And again, he grabbed my head and tried to yank it. I resisted in whatever way I could, but there he went, taking another horrid bite out of my cheek in a different spot. This time, he realized that I was irate, I couldn't hide it anymore, so he said he would park the car and be right back so we could go to the room. He sped away, and of course I never saw the asshole's face again.

You know what's the worst part? When I told my friend what happened, she said this stuff was normal. One time, a man bit her ass so hard that she couldn't work the rest of the day—and the bitch has liquid silicone injections, the good stuff, so imagine the pain. Then another time, a guy bit her chin so hard that she had to go home, again! Finally, an even worse story: Another friend had one of these fuckers bite her cock!!!!! I don't even know what I would do; probably nothing, that's what sucks about this kind of thing. Now, let me fantasize about throwing a solid punch, the kind that would make a bastard go deaf.

21.
WHEN IT'S TIME TO DO IT, I DO IT

I stepped onto the street at around 8 p.m. when not a lot of people were around; lots of trash everywhere, and I was essentially the only travesti. A Saturday during Carnaval, what else did I expect? I was trying to convince myself that it was worth it, but as soon as I set foot on the street, I wanted to turn back and go home. In less than an hour, I was bitten twice on the face by that disgusting old queen in boxer shorts (his bad breath still lingered on my skin and only came off with hand sanitizer; my eyes burned with rage, and the bite ached, the mark visible), and hundreds of cars passed me by without so much as acknowledging my hellos, my glances, me feeling like total garbage—and then came the asshole asking if I sold blow. He was annoyed when I said I'm not a top, and I don't cum, do or deal coke. "I'll look around and be back," he said. Can you imagine my face after an hour of putting up with his shit?

That's when a client appeared, the first real one of the night. He approached in a decked-out white 4x4 SUV, a big macho man with money, the same forty-something bald yet scruffy and paunchy guy that always shows up, just with a different face each time. He only had one question: if I kissed. You bet I do. I'm famous for it. He liked my answer and opened the door for me to settle in, then we agreed on thirty bucks in the parking lot.

He got to kissing right away—why bother brushing your teeth, right? Unreal. To this day, every single guy who wants to kiss me doesn't seem to care about oral hygiene, and I go on pretending it's all fine (I even carry a little bottle of Listerine in my bag because I'm considerate, but nada from them). His stubble was burning my skin, but he wasn't the worst kisser. We fit together nicely, his bad breath slowly dissipating from the intimate contact with my saliva—or, more likely, I was just getting used to it, growing immune to his smell.

We stayed like that for a long time until he decided to bring his cock to play while we were still kissing, as I clumsily juggled mouth-to-mouth and my hand found its way to his cock. For the blowjob, I immediately grabbed the condom, but when I tried to open it, he took it from my hand and said, "No, no, no need, it's just a blowjob." I asked if he thought risking an STD was worth thirty reais.

"But I don't have any STDs, you're the first travesti I've ever been with. I even think you're pretty much a woman . . . so pretty and so feminine. I don't have any STDs; you can take my word for it."

My jaw dropped all the way down to my cock. First, the piece of shit tried to stroke my ego by saying I *even* look like a woman, like that's a compliment! Not only is that a lame line but it also does nothing to entice me to take a stupid risk. But on top of that, he thought it was a good idea to say he'd never gone out with a travesti before, like we are the only ones transmitting diseases, never mind piece of shit men like him. Like we're all just born full of diseases that we are dying to spread! "I can suck you off too," he said. Oh, how cute, he trusts me.

"Honey, I won't do it without a condom. Get that into your head."

And you know what happened next? He grabbed my head with his strong, gigantic hands and pushed it onto his cock, telling me to suck: "Shit, when it's time to put it on, I'll put it on!" Imagine my panic. It was completely dark, which made it harder for me to even see the condition of his dick, but just having my nose near it while he forcibly rubbed my face against it, trying to get me to open my mouth, already told me everything I needed to know. What's funny is that under different circumstances, I might have liked the surprise of his funk, learning what his cock would smell like, taste like, only seconds before sucking–but this time, that was not the case. If I'd charged him in advance (I don't know why I didn't), I would have dogged him and run away . . . but I was afraid of not making any money on a cold, slow night, so I held firm, and even worse, I gave in. I ended up letting him put his cock in my mouth, just for a few seconds, while I unwrapped the condom.

When the condom was ready, I immediately stopped sucking and got away from his grip. Instead of cursing or punching the animal, what did I do? That's right, I kissed him. Despite everything happening, the desire to please him remained strong, fueled by the need to make sure he wouldn't regret the thirty reais he hadn't even given me yet. People often ask me why I didn't just tell him to go fuck himself, run home, or find another john– someone who would treat me better. I am not sure I have a solid answer, but I think I wanted to prove to myself (and to my comrades) that I was a good puta, capable of handling assholes and taking care of myself unless it was an extreme situation. But as it turns out, that's not how things really work.

(The Amara I am today has much wisdom to share with

her younger self. Yet I have also softened over time, and perhaps that younger Amara, with her foolishness and remarkable strength, has valuable lessons to teach me now, too. I am often torn between feeling sorry for her and feeling jealous, especially when I picture her fearlessly facing the world.)

Back to the car: We were kissing, making out, while I was struggling to get the condom on his dick. The problem was that with his cock hard, it was too thick, which made my job that much more difficult, but just by hearing the word *condom* it went a bit soft. With a dick that's getting hard, with the help of my mouth, I can make it work, but I can't do it with a dick that's going soft. In the hopes of getting it up again, and solving my problem, I did my very best, passionately kissing him on the mouth, as performatively as possible, but it still seemed he wasn't planning on coming anytime soon. He wanted more . . . and me, all innocent, thinking the worst had already passed.

Well, it wasn't enough, and he soon tried, with physical force, to force me to suck his dick without a condom (continuously reassuring me that he didn't have any STDs and telling me to trust him—I was the first travesti he'd been with, how could he have any diseases, right?), which was already hugely offensive and a massive violation. If that wasn't enough, when we got out of the car so he could fuck me standing up, in the bushes, he now hugged me from the back and tightly held my arms as he tried to convince me to let him bareback me, again with physical force.

He changed his tune here, and I had to listen to bullshit I'd never imagined I'd ever tolerate: If before it was "No condom, when it's time to put it on, I'll put it on," now he began to repeat "Let me put it in just a little bit, just the tip, when I'm about to cum I'll pull out." All for thirty reais! It wouldn't have been worth it even for three hundred! I tried my hardest to slip out of his grip, determined to not let his disgusting dick penetrate me or cream my ass (I tightened my butt cheeks as much as I could, not even a needle could thread through), and I only resisted screaming for help because I preferred to not lose face with my colleagues, even though I was all alone that night, and it was unlikely that anyone would come to my aid. The only thing I knew was that after this, I wouldn't have the mental capacity to keep working; I just wanted to disappear, forget the promise I'd made to myself about never going home in the red (again, wishful thinking).

Help came when I least expected it. The bastard went limp from my persistence. He softened up every time I brought out another condom (I used three to keep up his little game), and because of that, it took so much more work for him to try to get what he wanted. That is what kept me from hitting him, pitting myself against him (he was bigger than me, bigger than a mountain!), screaming for help, or just running away. He went limp and then, to keep him from going home all out of sorts, maybe to his wife (by the way, how could I not feel bad, picturing myself as an accomplice to what he was doing to his wife?), he asked me to at least beat him off so he could finish. And I complied, full of disgust, but I was just hoping to get this over with, the bastard still making me contort myself so I could fondle his asshole as I jerked him off (that was "his favorite," he told me).

He handed me fifty reais–like an extra twenty could possibly make up for what had happened. Before I got out of the car, he asked for my phone number, and still in shock, I gave it to him without understanding why. He said goodbye with a kiss on my lips, adding, "You're beautiful; this was great." Not an apology–definitely not from him. He probably didn't even grasp the enormity of what he had done, which only highlights the deep-seated issues we face ahead.

In *Captains of the Sands* by Jorge Amado, there's a scene where something similar unfolds, though in a more violent manner. The protagonist, Pedro Bala, rapes a virginal girl on a deserted beach and then, holding her hand, leads her to the other end to protect her from other boys. She cries the entire way, and when she's finally far enough away, she unleashes a stream of insults and runs as fast as she can. Meanwhile, the narrator paints a picture of a bewildered Pedro Bala, trapped in the sand and struggling to understand her reaction. He raped her, but in a society that dismisses and silences women–where her "No!" is conveniently twisted into a "Yes," and her pain is misinterpreted as pleasure–he remains oblivious to the gravity of his actions.

And it's not just Pedro Bala or this stupid client; all men are complicit in rape culture that begins in childhood. This is why men convicted of rape, even with overwhelming evidence against them, often cling to their innocence. They aren't monsters or exceptionally cruel; they are ordinary men raised to view the violence they inflict on women and travestis as normal. The issue impacts all women and travestis, though it disproportionately affects sex workers.

I didn't reflect on any of this while it was happening; it only came to me much later as I wrote about it. I remember going home that day feeling devastated and exhausted, waiting for a bus that never seemed to arrive, surrounded by throngs of partygoers enjoying Carnaval on that Saturday night. At first, I thought that his kiss, his affection, and the fact that he didn't haggle for a lower rate would somehow make me feel all right. But I wasn't okay at all; instead, I was overwhelmed by a deep, consuming despair. "Dead men don't rape," a phrase I once heard from a frustrated feminist, echoed in my head. Given how I felt that day, my client was probably lucky I hadn't found anything sharp in my pocket. In that moment, I had only one wish: to sever the pushy, superfluous piece of flesh that had no business growing where it did, bigger than it needed to be.

22.
WHAT DO SEX WORKERS WANT?

Even with normal sex, the most basic, everyday business, people will label it "filth" if it is something that more traditional Brazilian families—especially the patriarchs—might not be accustomed to. Nonetheless, the travestis are still here, along with the putas, too, and we are tired of being swept under the rug. How long will they keep pretending we don't exist, that this is not the only life available to us? I feel sadness, I cry, but don't expect I won't continue. The respectable family man loves to come and fuck, only offering us peanuts in return, but he hates that we dare speak our truths, that we kiss and tell to anyone willing to listen.

I started this work simply because I was horny. I felt lonely and desperate to be desired, touched, eager for someone to pay for my body. But I quickly discovered that it wasn't as fulfilling as I had imagined. Writing about it, using it for the material it provided, started to become the reason I did it. Now, I don't quite know anymore if I am a sex worker to write or if I write to do sex work, that's the truth. How else would you, my readers, get a glimpse behind the scenes of the world's oldest and most infamous profession if not for me? I have been interviewed left and right, invited to speak at universities, to participate in panels with politicians, and have been featured on the covers of prominent magazines and newspapers. It is no wonder—who else tackles this subject so openly, regardless of the consequences? Very few do this in Brazil, and even fewer are as bold as I can be.

But things are going to change. In these crônicas, obscenity will only appear from time to time, when a more respectable word falls short. Maybe then the family man won't take it so harshly when he appears in my pages.

23.
THIS PUTA IS A POET

ode to a blowjob

bitter moira fated amara
scat even after a shower
cock when it's looking for cunt
there's no point if it isn't fun
if it gets tough, you holler:
quéti like this there's no other
cheesy hole it's no bother
restless dick tongue on fire
hold on to the cock try harder
a girl can dream of better and higher

for the tenth time

trust me, i'm married,
blood donor, and hand to god,
you're the first
tranny i've been with, look
at my dick, how it drools,
not even if i give you another ten?
you look like you get tested
i did mine not even a month ago;
wedding band and all, it's true,
married, trust me.

short memory

i barely lie down and he's on top
thirsty unzipping his pants
doesn't put on that macho voice
doesn't show off his muscles, or
tell me he's one of the good ones:
he's in bed with a travesti
says it's the first time,
first time this month, maybe,
since he barely even needed any
lube, his asshole receives my dick easily

24.
ESCAPADES ON EASTER

In the beginning there was chaos—an overwhelming sort that leaves you feeling sorry. But then the dishes were washed, and the Goddess saw it and liked it. Next, the room was cleaned, vacuumed, and mopped with a fragrant cleaner, and the Goddess was even more pleased. Finally, I took care to cleanse the path from the rectum to the duodenum. Created an unobstructed path, and feeling two kilos lighter—the only benefit of douching, that sense of lightness—I stepped out into the night on an Easter Sunday, ready to resurrect a few things. Goddess who art in heaven, deliver me from evil today, will you? I need it in more ways than one!

It was time to put my anger toward men to the test. On Easter Sunday, the neighborhood was deserted, but no sooner had I gotten off the bus than a customer came up to greet me, "Blowjob is ten, yeah?" After a brief hiatus, I had already grown unaccustomed to seeing/feeling/having a cock in my hands/mouth. I accepted his offer almost out of habit, because I missed it, but not before playing that sweet little hard-to-get act that, by now, you all know too well. And it was worth it; I got showered with confetti. His nervous cock protruding from his pants, he wanted me to take it in my mouth right then and there, in the van while he drove, so I did. I even considered doing it without a condom, again because I was so eager, but I had to remind myself that this was work and not play. I had learned the importance of separating the two.

With the condom on, we barely made it to the end of the block: He got in my mouth, two thrusts, deep ones, the kind that cross your glottis and reach your uvula. In minutes, he was saying, "Slow down, slow down, I just came, you can just touch it lightly now." He left me at my corner shortly after, but not before saying no one knew he was there; oh, what a relief that he managed to escape from "his old lady's sharp claws" (his words, not mine)–the spirit of Easter must have been cursing the bastard. There was a time when I felt bad every time I met a married client because I didn't want to hurt their wives; but come on, it was just sex. And often mediocre sex at that. Maybe I was even helping those women; maybe they could barely stand sleeping with their husbands anymore. Now, I just hope they are doing the same, seeking somebody outside of the marriage, finding some pleasure. With a ten already in my pocket that morning, it was so much easier to start the workday.

It was chilly as usual, the clouds threatening rain, and there I stood in my spot by the speed bump. It was a great spot because cars had no choice but to slow down, and then their drivers would be forced to at least eye me, the merchandise. Most would drive right on by without looking at me, but many would make their decision by the time they'd stop: a little wave, "Come here, sweetheart," then the rest just sweet talking. My second client that night was like that. A nice big guy, kind of pudgy, with a fancy car; he was interested in the merchandise and asked for whatever I could do for thirty (I could do traditional full service in the parking lot). He paid me in advance, then got out of the car so I could do what I do best in the not-so-dark darkness of the parking lot (once I caught another travesti hiding nearby and watching me work in order to make fun of me, the nerve!). His zipper down, I couldn't resist, and I nibbled at it a bit just to get a taste of it–and oh, it was so good! And I quickly got up as I put the condom on.

He went a bit soft, though, once the condom was on, and so it was harder to get going (plus the latex of condoms tastes awful, a taste that truly stays in your mouth). But work is work, so I continued, going deeper, faster, then he started forcing my head with his hand. "Wait!" I said, "Unless you want me to throw up my dinner," as I took a breath. I wanted to keep going, but he did it again, forced me with his hand to take more than I could handle. After a lot of back and forth, me squatting in front of him, my calves started to cramp up. At one blessed moment, he finally asked me to get up so I could suck on his hairy nipple. He had bigger breasts than me by the way. Impressive. Nothing against hair, but sucking his hairy nipple was a total turnoff, and whatever horniness I had initially felt slipped away as hairs tangled in my teeth.

I didn't stop, though; I sucked his nipple as he excitedly touched himself. "So good," he said. I just wanted it to be over. When I got tired, I went back to squatting without asking for permission to do so, and then I found it easier to follow through to the end. I even managed to get aroused again. The pain in my calves wasn't as bad, compared to other options, but you could see the disappointment in his face; he would have rather had me suck his breast than his dick. In the end, he was all done, and I was still horny, and it took quite a bit of juggling for me to get my disgruntled cock back into place.

As I write this, it feels funny to me, a person so enlightened, so woke, to think of a kink as weird. Did sucking on his hairy nipples turn me on? No, not at all. But it was easy and comfortable, especially considering all the things I had endured as a puta (I complained about the pain in my calf, but when there was no pain to complain of, I found a new motive. Maybe it's like an addiction, and things are never quite perfect). Yes, his dick turned me on, and I wanted that feeling, but the main mistake you can make as a sex worker is to forget that it's not about the sex you want. You might get pleasure if you're lucky, but the important part is satisfying the client and quietly making your money (without pushing your limits, nor the clients', of course). If it's pleasure I'm looking for, I'm better off in a chatroom or the countless dating apps, right?

I remember a friend hated golden showers; she only liked conventional sex, missionary, even though she had to occasionally top. It didn't seem to matter that pissing on men is much easier, in theory, than penetration, and often even pays more. Another friend thought that foot fetishes were boring and hated when clients would show up in women's panties: She only wanted wild sex with capital *M* macho men, not realizing how much she could make if she entertained the others too. Our own prejudices keep us from easier, healthier, and more profitable sex work.

Will I live long enough to see the establishment of a professional course for sex workers? A classroom would be an ideal space for us to learn from mentors and from each other about the different aspects of sex and our own bodies. We need to understand how to care for ourselves—having sex multiple times a day demands special care, and it's unjust that we often discover these necessities by chance. We could also learn self-defense skills, which are crucial in a world as misogynistic as ours—teaching and sharing the secrets of our often-misunderstood profession.

25.
ONE YEAR OF AMARA, TWO LEVELS OF FUCK IT

There I was on the anniversary of my official debut as a travesti, as the travesti writing these words. It was May 1, 2014, a Thursday, the day of International Workers' Day, and a few days before the LGBTQ Pride Parade in São Paulo. I traveled to the city with nothing but women's clothes in my suitcase. I just bought them on credit at a famous clothing store through an installment plan that would take me almost a year to pay off. I started asking people I met, almost apologetically, if it was possible, and not too inconvenient, for them to maybe call me Amara. Some kind souls responded with "No problem," "Of course," and "Sure." That is how it all started—without me even realizing I was heading toward a place I didn't yet know I wanted to be. All I know is that at one point it took off, the word spread from one person to another until everyone was calling me "Amara" before I had the chance to introduce myself. It's hard to believe!

Nearly a year later, it was time to take stock. I wanted to see if asking myself "So what if I'm a puta?" had truly changed my life. This question became the heart of my blog, which eventually evolved into this book. Of the dozens of men I had sex with this year, some made me horny—especially the first ones—while others sparked nothing but indifference. In fact, many left me feeling the opposite of aroused. Yet every single one I met while turning tricks, within the confines of the world's oldest profession. It's sad to realize that all the sex I had this year was transactional, tied to money. It's sad because it makes me wonder: Am I not attractive enough, seductive enough? Have I denied myself the chance to enjoy a different kind of sex? I still feel terrified when I look at myself naked in the mirror, and I know that won't change overnight. I can't simply materialize as someone else. Part of me still craves validation from men who call me "beautiful" in bed, and perhaps the need for breast implants before attempting to enjoy sex, the unpaid kind.

Something I learned this year was the ability to just say *fuck it*, which I picked up from Indianarae Alves Siqueira and Monique Prada, two of the most important putafeministas I have ever met. I delayed my transition for as long as I could, waiting until I felt strong enough to face societal pressures. I feared I might have to sell my body for mere crumbs to survive, forced into prostitution overnight after being a virgin for so long–can you imagine? I had already built a solid reputation and earned the respect of my colleagues at the university, along with some financial independence from a scholarship. This made it easier for me to negotiate the terms of my transition, a privilege that many trans people discover when they transition after college, away from certain prying eyes. Initially, I envisioned a path to becoming a professor at a public university, securing tenure, and then boom! Become a travesti. But ultimately, I couldn't wait. With just a small sign of good fortune, I took the plunge headfirst.

What surprised me most was the horror I initially felt at the thought of becoming a sex worker. I delayed my transition for as long as I could, hoping to avoid this fate. But the moment I embraced my new identity, I went straight to the streets. Not only that, but I also began documenting every detail of my encounters with clients on my blog–two levels of *fuck it*. It was like the word *puta* had been tattooed on my forehead before I ever set foot on the streets. People see me as a travesti and immediately picture a whore; even in the unlikeliest of places, I am met with intrusive questions about prices, preferences, even acts (i.e., am I a top or bottom, do I swallow), a level of harassment I had never experienced before. It was maddening. Alongside it, I grappled with loneliness and a longing to truly belong to the sex-worker community–to not be seen as a tourist in a profession filled with others like me, where I am neither an alien nor aberration. Writing became an outlet. I am not great at making up stories, can't come up with shit, but my memory is sharp. I can't create fiction, but I can find a thousand ways to describe the sweetness of my pleasure, the bitterness of my pain. Finally, I had the opportunity to confront my fear of that "so what if"–what if that was me? Since others wanted to define me *that* way, since they could only see me *that* way–I radicalized.

I grew tired of fearing the road less traveled. I enrolled in college to avoid becoming a puta, so I could just have sex for free. But then I realized I was losing money by failing to embrace my talents and suppressing my desires. I am a puta travesti writer and a doctoral candidate in literary theory–two levels of *fuck it*, because I don't owe anyone an explanation. I am confronting my fears while living out my dreams. I know many people, a lot of people, would give anything to be as brave and liberated as I am now; as a puta, as if I were always meant to be: the puta, the travesti, the writer.

26.
MONOLOGUES OF THE TRASH

(part 1: before)
"You're a woman? Wow, I can barely tell! Juicy thighs, juicy butt, nice juicy lips . . . if it weren't for your dick, I couldn't tell. And how do you fuck a tranny? You do it all? I've never been with a man, but now I'm kind of into it. You top? Big cock? Ah, the hormones . . . but a hot tranny like you, it'd be a shame not to try. I don't even know if I can take it. I've never done it, but I want to know what it's like."

(part 2: after)
"Wow, you're beautiful, that was great . . . I'd even date you if you were a woman. Such a hot body, nice skin, pink lips, polite–but not like this, you understand? That chill husband-and-wife sex, the companionship, I would miss all that. It's not prejudice, it's just that I like women. I am crazy for pussy. You're good for a little variety once in a while, when I need a break. I am married, I love my wife."

This asshole comes to me pretending he's surprised I'm not cis ("a woman," in his dialect), thinking it's a compliment to say he "can barely tell," but still using masculine pronouns. The old "You do it all?" (he wants to know if I top). "I've never done this before," he continues (uh-huh, sure). "I'm not sure I can handle it" (really, you can't!?), then demanding a huge cock or it's "not going to happen" (and you've got to be hard 100 percent of the time). Rotten-assed queen, as I like to say: He likely knows every cock on the block but acts like he's a virgin. I don't even know what this one saw in me. I was just getting off the bus with a bunch of bags, heading to the boarding house to drop my things and get ready for work, but he didn't want to hear it. It had to be me and it had to be now. He treated me like garbage, but I ended up relenting to his requests because it's so much better to start out the night with cash in hand and expenses covered. So whatever came after that would be all mine!

We went to the motel, thirty reais for three hours, fifty for me (he paid at the end, I didn't manage to charge him beforehand). He was six feet tall, pudgy, already headed for the shower as soon as we walked in, while I undressed and stowed my bags in a safe place. He asked for a back massage. "You can go hard and smack my ass a bit too," he added. Hmm, I liked that; I was even getting turned on by the red marks on his skin, discovering a new sadistic side to me. He told me I was hitting him too hard, but I knew better than to listen.

At one point, he got tired of getting whipped and moved on to touching me, sucking me, doing every goddamn thing. But my dick refused to get hard. Finally, he gave up and asked me to suck him off. I did what I did best, but not as expertly or the way I would have if I were treated well. It was a job. I got him good and ready to fuck, but when we got down to it, his short stubby cock (thick, though), combined with his protruding potbelly, required maneuvers beyond my skill set: There was no way it was going to work, every time we moved his cock slipped out of my ass, and it hurt to get it back inside, especially with his ogre-like manners (and I was already sore from a botched douching, so this only made matters worse. Fast forward to the ogre I saw after that, who made me hurt the whole week).

With all the slipping in and out, at one point he ended up finishing, just like that–so anticlimactic, but it was better that way. These guys desperately need to learn how sex works, because whores also deserve better bedmates: It's amazing how little they know about how to please a partner, how much they think it's just a matter of sticking it in, even hurting us if possible. Some men don't care if you enjoy it, while others are very careful, but between those two types, there are those few who actually want you to feel pleasure, who want you turned on, but also who mostly put in minimal effort to make it happen. They assume we get turned on with a press of a button, that it's our duty to enjoy their pitiful attempts. I always imagine what the wives of such animals must go through.

He took another shower, while I was continuing to be so sweet, hoping he would pay me already, and wondering if I would be able to fuck again with my hole in this state. He delivered his monologue, the piece of trash–his performance laying bare his belief that I was desperate and foolish enough to want him as a side piece. Bet I deserve it, don't I? Serves me right.

27.
OBJECT OF DESIRE, ABJECT BODY

I recently came across comments claiming my blog posts were fatphobic. Revisiting them, I saw my writing in a new light, recognizing the prejudice I didn't even know I had. Perhaps unconsciously, I had channeled a twisted revenge on the difficult clients I'd dealt with, revealing the complexity of power dynamics and intersectional privilege. A fatphobic travesti—what a contradiction! Yet maybe it's not so surprising; we don't exist in a vacuum. I am responding to the very society that fosters fatphobia. While I edit the original posts, I revised a few lines for this book to reflect my growth without denying the conflicting perspectives I likely still hold. You can judge my evolution now.

This also prompts me to consider how sex workers, unlike other professionals, face unique prejudices and limitations in their line of work. It raises questions about what constitutes prejudice and how to deconstruct prejudice once we become aware of it. For instance, expecting cleanliness, bougie treatment, sterile and odorless bodies—is that elitism on my part? How many of you would be willing to suck on a cock that carries that "man scent," the smell of someone coming directly from a long day of manual labor, lingering even through the condom? There have been countless times when I have returned home, my face still heavy with that smell—along with traces of bad breath, alcohol, cigarettes. Some days, I relish it, as I share in these pages. But what about the other days when I simply can't get in the mood? In the best-case scenario, I might leave lipstick stains on their underwear as a form of revenge, or traces of my perfume on their skin, yet that risks losing a client, which ultimately solves nothing.

I meet workers after they leave their factories and construction sites, where they ask me to touch them for twenty or thirty reais before heading home to their families. To them, I am a reward after a long, grueling day. Does the fact that they pay me so little–though what does "so little" mean, considering what they make?–think of the poor widow's offering of two coins to Jesus in Luke 21:1-4, something to keep in mind–does that give me the right to at least demand basic hygiene? Or does my low price mean that I am obligated to accept whatever I am given? Even if I wanted to require cleanliness, where would my clients find the time or space to get clean? They come to me straight from work, often get with me in their car, or worse, behind bushes, seeking refuge in the shadows of our makeshift privacy.

Hairy balls, hairy chests–am I wrong for not liking that? Is it wrong to specify my preferences? There was that man who asked me to suck on his hairy nipples, his breasts almost as big as mine, though he didn't take hormones. He wasn't chubby; he was just fat. The word *chubby* is a euphemism that diminishes his *fatness*, reflecting our society's hypocritical attitudes toward body size. Was it prejudice on my part to feel this way? And more, to lose a boner at that exact moment, unaroused at the thought of sucking his chest and having hair in my teeth? And if that is the case, what am I supposed to do? I did my job, but half-heartedly. I let my boredom show until returning to his cock to suck with great gusto. After he finished, I noticed his embarrassment, as if he were ashamed of what he'd asked me to do—like seeking his own pleasure was somehow shameful.

Who among you reading this would allow yourselves to fuck, kiss, and truly feel—or at least pretend to feel—lust for every body overflowing in your arms? These are the bodies rejected by societal norms—much like mine, but in different ways. Nonconforming, resistant, neglected, crude, fat, hairy, disabled bodies that defy conventional ideas of masculinity and beauty. That are made to feel such little worth, shy, and oppressed. These are the bodies that can only be themselves in the presence of people like me, that can find comfort in beds like mine, needing acceptance for their desires in a world that excludes them otherwise.

Some people can only experience sexual arousal thanks to the work of prostitutes, and that's a direct result of normative beauty standards. To what extent is the existence of prostitution linked to this need? People often say there is something of Jesus Christ in every whore, and not without reason—he says that "prostitutes will get into the kingdom of God" (Matthew 21:31). But you know what? I don't buy that. We're not repentant Mary Magdalenes or hidden messengers of God; we are simply workers, earning a living through the sweat of our brows. Embracing pleasure—an inherently human pursuit often disrespected and dismissed—as a means of livelihood. And just you wait, my critique of social norms is only beginning: The language of this puta travesti writer will live freely or not at all.

28.
NOW YOU'VE EARNED YOUR TWENTY

I couldn't tell what he was looking for: a man in his forties, sun-beaten skin and eyes full of life's experience. He limped toward me, one leg shorter than the other, and perhaps because I was the first travesti he spotted, he stopped right in front of me. We engaged in endless chitchat, flattery, and flirting; I played along, though I really wanted it to end–there didn't seem to be any money in it. But then he invited me out for a beer, wanting to get to know me better. I had already made enough money for the night, so anything more would be a bonus. I accepted his invitation, even though I wasn't in the mood for drinking. I made it clear I wasn't looking for a boyfriend. As we walked through the neighborhood–a gender-nonconforming travesti and a disabled man, hand in hand–I couldn't help but wonder who people would notice first. Which of us would be deemed more unacceptable in their perfectly normative eyes? What would those who held hands in peace think of us?

He bought two beers at the bar around the corner, paying the steep prices typical of the area, and insisted on sitting at the most visible table outside for everyone to see. I played the part of a cheap ho, letting him kiss me right there for the price of a beer. My girlfriends walking by to make fun of me, yelling sarcastically, "Aren't you brave?" I couldn't help but laugh at the scene. Cigarettes, beer breath—he couldn't sit still, his body covered in menacing tattoos. It wasn't worth it, but I stayed. "Do you want a bump?" he asked. Me? The goody-goody? I didn't even like thinking about it. "It's cool, I should take the night off anyway," he said. "I've been doing too much of it. Listen, you're nice, polite, a good listener. I want to spend the night with you and have a nice time together."

"Well, not for less than a hundred reais, darling," I replied.

"I'll give you seventy!" he countered.

"Damn it, okay then . . . Where are we going?" The motel was about a fifteen-minute walk away and would cost another eighty.

We walked there around 8 p.m., the night cold and dark. I felt a knot of fear, worried that things might not be as they seemed and could take a turn for the worse, yet something made me believe I could trust him. We made our way downhill for twenty minutes through the chaotic traffic, the drivers cursing us. As we limped along the uneven sidewalks, which were hardly made for pedestrians, he tried to warm me with his awkward hugs, his affection both comforting and strange. When we arrived in our room, the first thing we did was take a shower, lather soap on each other in a joyful, playful way (at a certain point I turned off the shower, because you know I hate wasting water). Then we headed to bed, our bodies still damp yet smelling fresh, so our night could finally begin. We had agreed on seventy, but he started to negotiate for fifty, claiming he wasn't sure I would be worth the extra. Sourly, I retorted that fifty was the rate for an hour. We settled on fifty, and I got to work with a foul taste in my mouth.

In bed, the sweet gentleman from before transformed into an ogre. His hands forceful and hurting my breasts, pulling my hair, pinching and slapping my body. I worked through the pain, knowing there was little point in complaining. I was already hurting from the last client and had suffered in anticipation, imagining what would come next. Thankfully, his cock was tiny, swimming in the condom in fact, but I still worried. Seeing me in fear and pain aroused him; he liked that his itty bitty could hurt a professional, and he came right away. Afterward, he shifted back to his affectionate act, hugging me and sharing stories about the accident that had injured his leg, his tattoos, and his time in prison. He spoke of his run-ins with the police and dark tales of violence and drugs. He even claimed to have survived the infamous Carandiru Penitentiary massacre. I felt a twinge of skepticism at his words; was he serious? A shiver ran down my spine when he snapped at me, sensing my doubt. But he insisted he had turned his life around, saying his only remaining vices were cocaine and alcohol.

In the middle of our little chat, he grabbed my little breasts again, aroused. I told him our time was up, and that he had already got what his fifty reais covered. I moved toward putting my clothes back on, but he grabbed me, suggesting I take it easy. "Come here, let's have a bit more fun, there's no bad time with me." Before I could say anything, he was kissing me, groping me, doing whatever he wanted. I went back and forth between trying to resist and freezing like an inflatable doll. It made no difference what I did, or if I was into it or not. He pushed my head down to his cock for me to suck it, and as I grabbed a condom, he pried it out of my hand. At that point, I was afraid of not coming back alive; okay then, do as you wish. I was risking my safety for free, working overtime—but also a small part of me enjoyed the sheer lust in his eyes, and it didn't take long for him to cum again. Then he said, "Now you've earned your twenty; I'm satisfied!" Ah, so that's what I'm worth? At least it makes for a compelling title.

The rest of the night was calm, filled with conversation and cuddling as we tried to get to know each other. He ordered room service for us, saying, "See, there's no bad time with me, right?" He opted for a brand-name cognac while I had a soda. He chain-smoked in the closed room; despite the freezing cold, there wasn't even a blanket in that dump of a motel I once had thought was great. To find some warmth, I had to cling to that ogre the whole night, spooning in a haze of smoke. I was anxious to escape as soon as possible, knowing I had an early morning and a long day ahead, but I couldn't sleep a wink.

29.
THE MINEFIELD IN THE BUSHES

There were days when I came home with two reais in my pocket. Days I would suck someone off for ten just so I could escape the cold, days I would stay out all night hoping to make some cash, hours standing out there, lonely, alone, no self-esteem, feeling like shit. Days and days and days like this, until finally I hit the point where I went home in the red, having spent more than I managed to earn back. Dinner, water, the bus fare there and back, a locker for my things, a place to get ready: Out of the thirty reais we all spend on these things, I only managed to make back ten, which I accepted because I was horny more than anything.

A delivery driver arrived on his motorcycle, assuring me he'd be quick. I barely had to coax him; he promised it would take "less than ten minutes." I accepted, already envisioning how I'd write the story, perhaps drawing a parallel with the parable of the rich man and the poor widow I had mentioned earlier. Ten hard-earned reais he would have to explain to his boss as money for gas. I couldn't fault him for typical offers from wealthier men, who could pay more because they liked me, wanted to exploit me, or simply had money to spare. Along with his promise of a quickie, he had a steaming pizza waiting for delivery. "I only have a few minutes, I swear," he said, explaining he worked all night for forty bucks. I joked that this was more than I made most days—little did I know how true that would be for that day in particular. He then asked me to run to the boarding house to break a fifty for him. I wondered if it was all a bullshit scam, and if I should just keep the change, but the wafting aroma of pizza made his excuses seem genuine, so I decided to trust him. Off we went to the bushes.

He wanted my breasts, I let him touch them, suck them, even though it was more than he deserved for ten bucks. "I'm nice, see how nice this is?" he said, without noticing that he was hurting me, sucking too hard, nibbling too sharp. Funny how often that happens, clients thinking that they deserve a discount for treating us with (what they call) affection, for pretending to care about our pleasure; almost like they think they're doing us a favor by going out with us. But I let him get away with it, to go on believing that I liked it, and I pretended to enjoy him, his little pecker wanting to pop out of his underwear into my fingers, all playful (I'm hot and bothered now as I write this, remembering the scene). Then I bent down and started to slip on the condom, loose like a nightgown on his stiff cock; he was restless, eager to get it in anywhere he could. Already he was asking me to take it easy, moving it away from my mouth, and just as I was starting to enjoy it, in two or three seconds: "I came."

Only later, once our lust had faded, did we notice a strange smell invading our senses, coming from right beneath us—definitely not pizza. In the darkness, we couldn't see an inch in front of our noses, and the ground was so filthy it was better to steer clear, avoiding the risk of getting pregnant from the used condoms and who knows what else. He shrugged, climbed onto his bike, thanked me, and left. I dashed to the nearest lamppost, wondering if I had been the lucky one. Thankfully, I wasn't. A sigh of relief; nothing was stuck to the bottom of my heels. Thank goodness. If only that had been the worst part of the night, if only that had been my biggest problem . . .

30.
OH, IF THERE WERE NO RISKS!

From the perspective of radical moralism, women selling pleasure to men–negotiating that pleasure and putting a price on it–is indefensible. It's acceptable for a boss to make a profit and for a worker to perform under terrible conditions, but selling pleasure, and worse, enjoying it? That's unacceptable! No matter the negotiated price–whether it's fifty, one hundred, or five hundred reais an hour–critics will always label sex workers as victims, "exploited" by the so-called perverse men who are their clients.

For conservative radical moralists who parrot this logic, sex can never be seen as a service or good. You can't put a price on it, even though it's one of the most fundamental human needs. Still, there's no reason I should provide my best service for free. I seize every opportunity to take money from a man; it's one of my greatest joys in life. In moments like this, I can't help but think of Georgina Orellano, an Argentine sex worker and one of the most inspiring activists I've ever met, who said, "If I can't get paid for sex, this isn't my revolution."

I'm sorry for those who think otherwise, but I would rather raise the voices of sex workers, listen to our own stories and demands, and fight for better conditions and full autonomy to choose our paths–including the choice to stay in prostitution–instead of those who claim to know better or speak on our behalf. No one in their right mind really believes they'll ever see the end of sex work. The priority, then, is to advocate for safer practices, better pay, and to eliminate the weight of stigma surrounding the profession.

The fear that these people feel, we know what it is: The less violence involved, the less stigma attached, the more women will begin to give themselves the right to choose to work sex, choosing to profit from the pleasure of men (and in the not-so-distant future, even from other women). Whether it is to cover a single bill, buy something they desire, a gift, go out on the weekend, or make it their main source of income, imposing the value they desire, a value that allows them to live, not just survive. Yet this moralism refuses to accept a woman who freely chooses to profit from men's lust to sustain herself, to satisfy these desires, fantasies, and needs, a woman who finds in sex her professional fulfillment.

In the end, who is truly exploited when sex work is performed without the threat of violence, free from stigma, and with proper dignity and compensation? I dream of the day when the word *puta* is no longer a slur; a day when people won't even understand why it ever was. But that day is still far off. Today, we face a feminism that claims to be radical yet aligns itself with the Catholic Church and the fundamentalist factions against sex workers' rights. It's time to advocate for a feminism that legitimizes our agendas and takes our struggles seriously–a putafeminismo, since mainstream feminism, Feminism with a capital *F*, continues to overlook us. May this book help pave that path.

31.
WHERE'S THE CONDOM?

At first, I was fine to give head without a condom if it was with the men I wated to have sex with–just head, not penetration, Goddess forbid! Sex was damn good back then, when I was still so new to being Amara, still so insecure in my body, dying to get a compliment. When I was desired, I desired in return, it was that simple. With that, I experienced the pleasure of tasting every bit of every man with my five senses–I even used my hearing, the sounds you hear, priceless! I didn't get any STDs thanks to PrEP, the hepatitis A and B vaccine, and my dumb luck, but it was better to curb risks before it was too late–to teach those bastards a lesson, especially because none of them were worth the risk. And so began the Rubber Age, my penis hat era, and the end of pleasure.

Since I started Androcur (a testosterone blocker), anal was always painful, and it got worse with the anal fissure I still hadn't realized I had. My prostate was literally a pain in the ass, long gone the pleasure it used to provide. All this plus all the shitty behavior from the assholes I met and having to suck on condoms, it was enough to turn sex into something terrible, bland, mechanical on a good day. So to return myself to a little pleasure, I stopped taking blockers for roughly two months to see what would happen, and I noticed the effect right away. My libido came back, my erections; my asshole throbbed, begging to be filled. Once again, I felt a desire to make my whole body generate pleasure, like the giant sexual organ that it was. It was in this context that I went back to the streets, ready to make buckets of cash and gorge on juicy flesh to boot.

As soon as I stepped out, that delivery driver on the motorcycle from last time showed up, now offering fifteen instead of ten for the full package and not just oral. I'd gone out late that night, it was already around ten, and I needed to start making money as soon as possible, even if it meant pulling an all-nighter, so I accepted. He needed to take a piss first, water the plants behind the bushes, so I came up to him from behind, held his little guy in my hands, and said, "Okay, go ahead." You think it would behave? Naughty little thing got hard immediately, his owner struggled to keep its focus, make it work, unsure at this point which function was more urgent—his cock seemed ready to move on as piss deliciously sprayed out.

Once he was done, I put the condom on him, knelt down in my high heels, and started my favorite part of the job. It didn't last long, just like last time, but now he came at me with something different: "Turn around, or I'll cum too fast." I nodded. While I smeared myself with lube, his cock went soft in my hands, until the condom looked more like an oversized boyfriend sweater. We tried to put it up my ass anyway, the little thing almost going in then slipping out, bending where it shouldn't. He pulled out long enough for me to use the opportunity to smear on more lube, to see if it would help get him hard, make this easier—then I felt a strange texture, a viscous fluid in my hands. I found myself asking, already knowing the answer: "What's that, love?"

"I came."

I continued massaging him, amused by the whole thing, while he still trembled. Soon I felt something again in my hands—how strange, oh wow, how is this possible? I froze—the condom!? The unusual texture wasn't just because of his cum but because I was touching his bare skin! I spun on my heels, ready to push him back onto the asphalt, when something shifted inside me, and I felt some kind of goop running down my leg: His little pecker having been dwarfed by the condom and with an asshole as tight as mine, his member had come out and left the rubber behind. Hanging from me like a pony's tail with his load now dripping down my leg. I was overwhelmed with relief that he hadn't taken it off on purpose—though he didn't notice anything in the dark. Come back again, love! On to the next.

32.
PLEASE STOP, I CAME HERE TO FUCK

It took some time, but he finally arrived: a handsome Prince Charming on a gleaming white horse. Through his words, gestures, and gaze, he spoke volumes, said things like "You're too pretty to be here; your skin is so white," and "I'll rescue you from this life and take care of you, you'll see." He was relieved my parents "didn't know what I did at night" and that I only did it "a little," making it easier for me to leave it all behind. He promised to help me save money; for my breasts, even, too. He felt too good to be true. He showered me with compliments and masturbated himself with perfect harmony, like a maestro conducting a symphony, his desire inflamed by the thought of saving me from my own grim reality. I had to hold his hand and insist he slow down; otherwise, he'd cum right then and there, in the car, and then goodbye to my money. Eventually, he relented to my charm, and we moved to a room–though not before he made me promise to take care of him and give him a real chance. And I did. I only charged him forty reais, the exact amount I needed to cover my expenses. His cock had the largest head I had ever seen–almost mushroom-like. I felt a sharp pang of anticipation, already envisioning the impalement, despite having practiced with a dildo all week.

Naked in bed, making out, working his condom-covered

cock with my tongue, I was having fun seeing his pleasure, feeling like a total actress. He pulled me close and started kissing me, caressing me, his beard scratching my face. Until, out of nowhere, he went, "Hey, wow, whoa, what's that, girl?" That's when he saw me in all my glory, out and proud, if you know what I mean. I had stopped taking the testosterone blocker, so there it was, horny, and I laughed at his reaction. I followed my instinct and touched his body, his balls, taint, ass, while he touched himself everywhere, speaking in the funniest monosyllables–"huh," "oh," "yeah," "ow," "no, "ouch," "uh," mouth and eyes saying one thing and then contradicting each other, until, ahem, finally, "You can do whatever you want to me." Any travesti worth her salt knows what that means: "Do whatever you want" is a euphemism for "Come fuck me." So I went to massage his hole, making sure I got it right.

"No, no, oh, I came here today to fuck you, please stop." That is what his words conveyed, but the language of his hands told a different story–agitated, rushed, about to cum at any moment. I decided to poke the bear: "Come here and fuck me then, if that's what you want." And then, "Enough romance, someone will knock on the door any moment now." I just had to open my damn mouth, didn't I. He prepared to fuck me, smearing lube on my asshole, getting ready to dig deep.

It hurt, I admit. The pleasure I had felt earlier had faded, but the evening was easier than I'd imagined. Once his head was in, the rest of his cock slipped in without almost any friction, and we stayed like that, with him insatiably moving in and out, until he closed his eyes, and he latched on to my pain. His pubic bone pressing against me before he collapsed onto me without warning.

Afterward, he slipped into the usual routine of amnesia and haste. He just had time to ask if I had change for a fifty–late as he was for his next appointment–before he vanished, forgetting all about saving me from my supposedly horrible world. Typical men.

33.
SEX UNDER THE MOONLIGHT

Cars with tinted windows opened just a crack; only eyes were visible, though they took in all of me. I waved, flirted, beckoned them closer, as my heart raced with fear and anxiety at the thought of them stopping. Then the usual song-and-dance would play out: "Little trick, love? Blowjob is twenty, thirty for full service in the car." I even considered lowering my prices to attract more clients, but everyone I offered a discount, five reais less, would reply: "Good to know, I'm just having a look around." Fourteen years ago, when I was almost seventeen, with my allowance in my pocket, I once inadvertently wandered down a street downtown where sex workers kept their posts. One of them stopped me and invited me to go upstairs; a lightbulb flashed in my mind. How much? She charged twenty-eight. I went with her though I didn't have change, so I gave in to paying thirty. At that time, I was at the peak of my foolishness, desperately trying to be the man everyone expected me to be. In my attempt to appear grown-up, I saw it as an opportunity to lose my virginity. I remember being shocked by how low her price was. What hurts is seeing that, fifteen years later, my rates–and those of every travesti here–are even lower. Fifteen years later.

This time, my client arrived on foot. Every night, countless men pass by–men who seem unsure of why they're walking by, heads down, shamefaced yet excited by the experience. They move quickly, visibly nervous, stealing furtive glances from the corners of their eyes. They pretend not to notice us but always stop at the first sign of acknowledgment. "Little trick, love?"

"What did you say? Ah, a trick. I'm just going for a walk." They must believe we're out here simply because we have nothing better to do, eager to have sex with them for free.

Not this one. It was on his third pass that I finally hooked him. I'd already made enough to cover the night, so anything he gave me would be profit. In the end, I accepted even less than I had anticipated, just to take home a little extra cash. "You got a big dick?" I asked. "Ah, it's nothing." Nothing. I can't imagine what "big" must mean to him, then. It's like men with big dicks take pleasure in pretending they're not *that* big; they enjoy seeing a sex worker surprised. I was lucky I was already greased up from the previous client, I just needed a little extra lube to make him slip right in.

It was quick. He paid in advance, and I used the flashlight on my phone to verify that the bill was indeed a twenty. I then grabbed a condom, hung my bag on a steady branch of a nearby tree, and knelt down, unzipping his pants. With his cock all wrapped up, I started blowing him, going as far as I could, getting him nice and ready so I'd suffer less. Still, I suffered. Having sex standing with nothing to lean against wasn't exactly my preference–especially in the dark, unsure of what I might be stepping on. Suddenly he pulled me up from below, turned me around, and started rubbing against my ass, testing the waters. He tested so much that he ended up going in, but not before I added more lube. I was already chafed after the mushroom I had earlier, and this one was uniformly thick, so it hurt even more, but at least he came quickly.

When he pulled out, it was so dark I could barely see if the condom was okay–poor visibility, the client in his usual post-orgasm rush. They cum and then want to vanish as soon as possible, but still neither of us wanted to accidently touch any shit that might have come out. Sometimes there's some on the dick or condom when it exits your guts. What else would it be, flowers? Luck– that's as much as I can ask for as a prostitute working in the dark, in the bushes. Far from the places some of my colleagues get to work: luxury hotels with bathrooms for basic hygiene, running water, clean sheets. Sometimes all we have is our faith.

34.
YADA YADA, BODY ODOR, IN AND OUT

There's nothing quite like a great day at work. I barely had time to get bored or down; money came easily, with one customer after another. I enjoyed playing the romantic, full of seduction—my first time in a semi truck. Not in the back, but in the cabin; still, who wouldn't want that? It wasn't even seven yet when I hit the streets. A few cars passed by, and I was bracing for the worst when the first one finally pulled up. A shy, chubby guy with a nice beard, probably in his early forties, reached out with rough, strong hands, pleading for affection. His scent reached me even from a distance. We chatted for a few minutes while he weighed his options, eventually making it clear that he was uninterested in a quickie in his car. "You okay with a love motel? I want to be able to take my time—at least an hour and fifteen," he said. Totally fine by me! I thought it was hilarious that he so graciously suggested "an hour and fifteen." We settled on forty reais and headed to the motel. I gently caressed his little guy, keeping it light and friendly, and over the pants. "Will you let me take care of your big cock?" I asked. "It's small," he said. "Let's see if it won't get huge once I put it in my mouth."

The redeeming thing about this motel was its bathroom and shower, which he rushed to as soon as we arrived. While it didn't solve everything, his stench still lingering sour and strong—it certainly improved things a little. We got naked in bed, rubbed against each other, and since I didn't know what kind of script he was looking for, I prepared to suck him off and reached for a condom so I wouldn't be tempted. There are times when, oh, I am desperate to taste it, to feel it in my mouth. Where's a boyfriend when you need one, I'm horny here!

I used my tongue to unravel the condom onto his dick. I felt him harden little by little, my hands free to massage his balls and to make their way over his taint to the rim of his asshole. I was curious to see if he was into it. He is! His body relaxes more and more as my fingers touch his G-spot, and I gently massage the area. With the condom secured, I start to explore his groin with my mouth, licking, kissing, sucking. I get to his scrotum and politely stop there to nibble at first and then swallow it whole, now one ball at a time, tracing each testicle delicately with my tongue, applying light pressure, while he jacks off in delight.

Then he suddenly pulls me away and looks at my mouth with an expression of doubt. He kisses my shoulder, neck, ear, cheek, chin, not knowing if he should (or can) venture near my mouth. He finally works up the courage and attacks my mouth, not quite sure what to do there, kissing chaotically. Teeth brushing must not be a staple in this client's daily routine, but given how prevalent bad breath is, I kissed him anyway and however he wanted. In the meantime, he moved his hands as if I couldn't see them, playing with a kind of reckless abandon, going for my dick, trying to revive my dick, as dead and buried as it was.

It felt nice, I won't lie, but getting my cock hard is hard work. I tried using my imagination to wake it up. At one point it worked: While massaging his asshole, I imagined fucking him while he touched me, and my cock responded. He noticed and immediately straddled me, trying to keep me hard at all costs. I moved to get the condom, but before I could unwrap it, my cock returned to the land of the dead.

He sensed that it wasn't my thing, and stopped insisting without complaining. I returned to his dick to suck him off while he laid back like a king, savoring the moment. I moved my fingers around his rim, massaging his balls, sucking his cock deeply, only pausing to use my tongue to encircle its head. Suddenly, without warning, he froze in ecstasy, and came, naked on the bed. I had only been at it for forty minutes–if that–and I had expected him to want a little more, especially after his initial "at least an hour and fifteen, so I can take my time" request. But no sooner than I could curl up in his muscular, virile arms and rest a little did he utter: "We're here on your terms, okay? I know you're working, so whenever you want, we can go." Men. He barely came a moment ago, and already the romance was dead. So be it. Off I went to make more cash.

35.
YOU'RE WAY
TOO HOT

I thought I must have misheard it—maybe it was just in my head—but it rang out clearly: "Hot man," "Wow you're such a hot man." The word *man* echoed in my ears, unmistakable, repeated several times. It was, of course, meant as a compliment, but it was the furthest from. It stung like an insult. He was well-dressed, chubby, and hairy. The word *gallant* came to mind—I've always had a fondness for those old-fashioned terms. He had rented a car at the airport and showed up for a bit of fun before his next flight. And somehow chose little old me. He asked for my price and told me to get in the car. Without telling me exactly what he wanted, we headed for the motel.

Time was tight, but he still wanted to shower before climbing into bed. I silently appreciated his thoughtfulness. His cock was impressively massive in every way imaginable; just looking at it, I feared the worst, salivating and moaning, "My poor asshole!" I asked what kind of sex he wanted. "The full service is fifty, right?" he said. "Here's the money, come here." So I got into bed, anticipating the pleasure and pain of impalement; my mouth watering from all that beauty. A delightful big boy, as my grandmother would say!

With his dick properly wrapped—*wrapped* is such an odd word to appear next to *dick*, right?—I start sucking him off. He could barely fit into my mouth, but necessity—the mother of lust—helped me find a way to swallow it whole. It took a few minutes and many positions; as he grabbed me and kissed me, we made out for a bit, lust all over his face, then he started with his "compliments."

"You're such a hot man," he said. I filled with rage. He continued to insist that he didn't have much time and promised to come back another day. I hardly heard him as I withheld my urge to slap him. Then he decided to grab my body and hungrily took the joystick between my legs into his mouth. He didn't hold back; mouthed me without a condom. But there was no indication that it would perk up, even though I was horny. Who knew what my problem was—sometimes it's like it only works when it shouldn't, or when I don't need it to.

He glanced at his watch, looking flustered. "It's almost time for my flight, and I'm still here," he said as he stumbled to get dressed; his horniness wasn't helping, his mouth still on my candy bar. I took off the condom and started to jerk him off, and he looked like he was close, then suddenly, he pushed my hands away.

"No, no, no, I'll come later, when I get back from my trip," he shrieked.

"As you wish, champ; it makes no difference to me."

He jumped out of bed and hurriedly got dressed, a bit clumsily, burning hot from within. Before he left, he slipped me another twenty—the change from the motel—and dropped me back at my usual spot on the street, screeching away for the airport. I considered calling it a night, but just then, another client rolled up: a truck driver who invited me to join him on a trip through rural Brazil. Come with me?

36.
THE TRUCK MOTEL

His semi truck had been parked there for a while, the driver peering out through the tinted window. By that point, I had already seen two clients, my pockets full of cash, and was seriously considering heading home when he waved me over. I approached his truck, my heart racing; I had never done anything like this before. As I stood outside his truck, even in heels, I felt tiny next to his large, laughing head sticking out the window. (Though to be honest, I can't quite recall if I was wearing heels that night. But I probably was, and it does make for a better story.) "Why do you look so startled?" he asked, amusement dancing in his eyes. The way he looked down at me felt strange, his head hovering high above. "I'm a bit wary," I replied. "Nonsense!" he chuckled, launching into small talk, trying to put me at ease. My patience was already wearing thin.

"Little trick, love? I can't stay here chatting all day, I got bills to pay . . ."

He seemed to understand how things worked in the neighborhood, yet he played dumb. He asked about my prices and talked some more while I considered walking away. Finally, he decided; he wanted a blowjob. "No problem, *mon chéri*, if you have cash," I said. Climbing into the truck cabin—wearing those heels I can't quite recall—felt like an adventure, a bit of a challenge. I was afraid I would twist my ankle trying to hoist myself up, while he seemed to relish the drama. Once I finally managed to get inside, I had to slam the door several times to get it to close. Then he asked me where we were headed, as if he didn't already know. "Right here, no?" I replied, realizing the truck was far too large to park anywhere near the love motel, let alone the boarding house. This was already feeling like too much work for a quick blowie. It sucks that I have to subject myself to this as a travesti sex worker. Many cishet men would never admit that they are attracted to travestis, seeking us out for blowies because "we do it on the cheap" or at least less than what most cis women charge.

Once we finished the awkward back-and-forth– "Where are we going?" "Nowhere"–he grabbed a piece of cardboard from behind his seat, one of those makeshift windshield covers that block the heat, and propped it up on the dash. The tinted windows hardly needed extra cover, but there it was. Voilà, a makeshift love motel. He even reclined the seat so we could use it as a bed. It was nice and dark, and I started to touch him affectionately. He looked pleased, even complimented me. I helped him out of his clothes, peeling them off his stocky body, his pronounced gut, his sunburned, unshaven skin; he looked to be a traditional Brazilian family man. And then he asked me to take off my clothes too. I hesitated. "It's just a blowjob, babe, really quick." "Ah, but it'll turn me on," he insisted. I ended up giving in to see if I could speed things up. I grabbed the condom, opened it, and started practicing my technique of putting it on with my tongue, without hands. But his dick was too soft for that to work.

Once the condom was on, I started sucking him off. His rough, callused hands rubbed against my face, my neck, my tits, messing up my hair. That kind of touching was worth a lot more than twenty reais! And it annoyed me. A little chub was the best I could get from him, and he didn't even seem to mind, as if he already knew his body well enough to expect nothing more. He called me beautiful, professed his love, and asked me to travel all across Brazil with him in his truck, all while his eyes remained closed, lost in his own little imaginary world. His mini erection showed no signs of improvement.

I traveled down his pants to swallow his balls, one at a time, then two at once. They were clean at least, despite all the hair. He howled in the cabin, writhing, convulsing. I wasn't sure if his reaction was from pleasure or pain, though he assured me he was very pleased. That was the only time his cock got hard, though as soon as I let go of his balls, his dick deflated, and his semi returned. I decided to explore other options since my position was straining my neck, and his convulsions were becoming too much. Honestly, the type of men I come across! I massaged his taint, then lightly put my finger inside, while he jerked off his semi-erect cock–again without indication this would end soon.

Time was running out; my impatience growing, I asked him to hurry up because I was already working overtime for free. He asked me to go back to his balls, and I did; he lay flat out on the seat, masturbating madly, the condom already off. I had never seen anyone so horny for ball play! After some time he finally came, and made quite the mess! He then lay there exhausted, lifeless. I played with his cock, grabbing it with my fingers and gently pushing it up from the base to try to get out that last bit of cream. It was nice to see that soft dick in my hands, and its white droplets coming out, one by one. We used toilet paper to clean him up, then it was time to settle up. I received an extra ten for my dedication. The funny part was that he continued to be affectionate even after he finished, talking about taking me on a date and whisking me away with his truck to explore Brazil. Who knows, maybe someday. I won't lie; it was an intriguing idea.

(P.S. Days later, while I was writing this, he called again to ask me out–can you believe it? He even came to pick me up near my house last night. That story comes next.)

37.
TOO MANY TRUCKS FOR TOO LITTLE SAND

It's striking to see those big, brutish men—rough hands and all—transform into fragile little creatures in my presence. They become such needy boys, craving a bit of love or simply someone to lend an ear. It's amusing but also dangerous; we all know how they react to rejection, especially from someone like me, a puta travesti. In those vulnerable moments, they reveal parts of themselves they wouldn't dare show their own shadows. A simple "No, thank you" can ignite hostility, even violence. "What do you mean you aren't into me? Who the fuck does this puta travesti think she is?" Women's bodily autonomy—cis or trans—faces constant threats in society, especially in spaces like this, where our worth is often diminished even further. We're expected to be grateful for whatever scraps we receive, and any misfortune that befalls us is seen as our own fault.

I had a moment like this with my truck driver. Anxiety set in as we drove through my neighborhood; he had picked me up before I even got to work. He refused to let me negotiate over the phone, leaving us somewhere between thirty (his offer) and fifty (my counter). "We'll settle it later," he said. I hesitated, remembering a girlfriend's warning: "If you let these assholes pick you up in your neighborhood, they'll start showing up at your house, your school, talking to your neighbors." I had chosen a spot far enough from my home, though still in the same area, so I thought I was safe. I hoped I was safe.

From the start, he showered me with declarations of love. "You look so beautiful," "I missed you," even though I was sweaty and disheveled after teaching until nearly 9 p.m. I volunteer as a literature professor, a passion of mine alongside sex work; few places would dare hire a travesti like me. Mystique was out the window as I arrived with books under my sleeve and a little stubble on my face–not just peach fuzz anymore. Yet none of that seemed to faze him. I lied, claiming I taught history full-time at a public school and worked as a puta only to fund new breasts, which was why I never worked during the day. He liked that story, insisting I didn't need new breasts–I was beautiful as is, but if I really wanted, he could help. They all say that. But when it comes time to pay me for my labor, they always want a discount. You see how it is?

Then, he started saying how he so badly wanted love, a relationship, something more serious.

"But that's not how this works, my dear," I replied. "Have you even wondered if I'm interested in all this love you're offering?"

"Are you?"

"No, I like my freedom."

"But you can keep working, get with whoever you want . . . What if it's like that?"

"Nuh-uh."

"Ah, so we can't go out because I want a real relationship, not just one of your tricks."

It would have been one thing for him to proposition me over the phone; I could have simply agreed and sent him on his way. But hearing it alone in the cabin of his truck on a deserted road–somewhat close to where I lived–felt entirely different, especially before he had even paid me. Of course, he took the opportunity to get close and touch me. They think we're naïve, claiming they want a relationship and that they'll "let" us keep working, but what they really desire is sex on demand–nonnegotiable. What can you do in a situation like this? I don't know; I gave in. I let him touch me, kiss me, I tried to look normal, horny, but fear was gnawing at me from the inside.

I got undressed, afraid someone might show up at the end of the road, that he would become violent with me or abandon me there. In all this excitement and flurry, we started to have sex–just the oral kind. His cock was still soft as I put a condom on him with my mouth. I had improved my technique, so it worked no matter the state of erection. And went straight for his balls–licking, sucking, swallowing, even if they were sweaty. He howled with pleasure like last time, writhing violently, stretching his legs. I struggled to anticipate the wild flailing of his limbs, nearly getting kicked in the process–but that was the only way his cock would get hard. If I stopped, it went limp, immediately. So I focused on his balls, occasionally attempting a little graze of his semi-hard dick; that pretty much summed up our entire hour together. Sometimes I fingered his hole, just encircling the rim, to see if it would help. It did, but only the slightest bit. My jaw was tired, my throat sore from going so deep, so I hoped he would cum soon. My eyes were watering, my nose was runny, and I was gagging a little bit from when I went a little too far. If you think blowjobs are pretty to watch, you might have only watched them through porn. In real life, they are an ugly mess! Even for someone who is generally a fan. I love giving head to someone I like–sweat, scent, and all–but this one was too much.

As time wore on, and he still hadn't cum, I stopped suddenly and said: "Honey, you haven't even said how much you were paying me, and it's been too long. We are done." He responded through an exhale: "It is going well, isn't it?" and promised he would finish soon. He asked if I could just suck on his balls a little bit longer while he jerked off. With the tips of his two little fingers he rubbed the head of his cock, his fingers like tweezers, the opposite of what I was doing with my full hand wrapped around the entirety of his soft cock. He came easily. Thick milk splattering all over his belly as he lay in his truck. I sat there, disheveled, thinking how funny it is that we each have our own unique ways of cumming, finding pleasure—ways that not even God could work around. Going out with a sex worker can give clients a chance to explore new things, discover new ways of enjoying their bodies, gain some much needed sex-ed. But in practice, many men seek out prostitutes primarily for an escape from the pressures of everyday life and the repressions they are subjected to. They often approach their time with us as a fleeting moment of relief rather than an opportunity for self-discovery—not much room for deeper connection and understanding. It's a pity; we could offer so much more.

And that's exactly what happened here. After he finished, he cleaned himself up with toilet paper while I hurried to get dressed. I tried to assert my right to the fifty reais I was owed, but he hit me with his rehearsed nonsense: "You'll leave me broke at this rate," and "I treat you so well." The audacity! In the end, I settled for thirty just to get rid of him. I asked for a ride back to my neighborhood, and prepared for my twenty-minute walk home. As I walked, I felt a wave of relief to be alone again in a familiar place. Better to forget about that trucker.

38.
A PUTA IN EUROPE

I didn't want to leave the Netherlands, where I had just spent the last four days as a guest of a sex workers' rights international organization, all expenses paid, without at least getting a taste of the dick and the dough of a European man, especially with the exchange rate. Since it was illegal for me to proposition clients on the streets of Amsterdam, I downloaded one of those hookup apps and created a profile. Imagine my disappointment when I realized the app was primarily filled with muscly men eager to flaunt their biceps and six-packs. Despite that, I decided to stick around. I chose the sexiest, most feminine photo of me and posted it with the caption "male enough?" In the description, I wrote, "Brazilian tran$$exual woman looking for some fun."

As soon as I submitted my profile, my phone buzzed with messages—so many that it became hard to respond. I had to specify that I was looking for cash, that I was an escort, and not on the app out of sheer lust, even though I was intrigued to get to know all these bodies. I arranged several meetings with men, in my hotel even, but something seemed to always get in the way. After two days of this, I decided to meet someone just for the thrill of it—for the pleasure, not the money—so I wouldn't return home with only my thumb in my mouth.

I made plans with a guy, finally. The English he wrote in messages to me was so chaotic, even more than mine, that I figured he must not be Dutch (in the Netherlands, English is basically a mother tongue). As the early morning approached, the cold biting and the sky threatening rain, I headed out in my overcoat–the one I hoped would help me pass through Dutch immigration without any issues, disguising my transness: How naïve I was!–on my fifteen-minute walk to meet him. Arriving at our spot, I watched him pass by, pretending not to know me. I was confused, wondering if I had been mistaken, but moments later, he returned, awkwardly ushering me to his apartment just a block away. He signaled for silence on the way, as we climbed the stairs, and I started panicking a bit, knowing I hadn't told anyone I was there. I wanted to go back to my hotel–the messy situations I get myself into! When we got to the apartment, the bastard explained why he had to pretend not to recognize me: There was a guy nearby who couldn't see him with me because no one in the neighborhood knows he's into "these things." For this reason, the silence.

Dutch? No, Algerian, he told me. We switched from English to Spanish at his request. He started to take my clothes off, touch my skin, tell me I was "muy bonita," that he liked trans people like me, young, not the ones over thirty. Dumbass. I laughed to myself because I was already thirty then, even though I said on the app that I was twenty-two. It can be our secret! He then started to whimper about how there was likely "no chance without a condom, right?" to see my reaction. I was pissed; you can barely tell the difference between the idiots here and the idiots over there, it doesn't matter the continent. I said, "No, of course not," somewhat emphatically, and he pulled the whole "Mejor así, peligroso," like he agreed. Sure.

The sex was a mess. He kept changing positions, each time wanting to try weirder and weirder stuff and subjecting me to it. I let him play with my body as he wished. Amara the contortionist. I admit I felt a bit of a boner from feeling used, but that was hardly working with him. Eventually I grew tired and suggested he take it from there. It was hurting me, and he said, "Okay, okay, what if we tried taking a bath, doing it between your thighs?" It was my first time experiencing something like this–slippery from soap and water. He put his cock in the gap between my thighs and kept going at it like an idiot for a few minutes until he came, almost without warning. Have you ever seen cum when it comes in contact with hot water? Trust me, you don't want to. It's sticky like glue, and nothing can make it come off!

We ended up having a bit of a chat, discussing "homophobia" in Brazil, the Netherlands, and Algeria. He was shocked to learn that in Brazil we could live our lives openly on the street, kissing on the mouth and everything, without it leading to jail. When I told him I did sex work, he was really curious to know more–where I worked, the police situation, the violence, and my parents? But I was too tired and just wanted to go back to my hotel. I had a packed schedule ahead–the last day with sex worker activists from around the world with little old me representing Brazil. As I was leaving, he mentioned that two travestis were staying on his floor; he was unsure if they were Brazilian or Colombian, and if it weren't so late I would have knocked on their doors to talk a bit. Just as I was about to head out, he casually reminded me to put on my damn overcoat so no one would be able to tell that I "wasn't a woman." Asshole.

39.
YOUR GIRLFRIEND
FOR FIFTY AN HOUR

En route for a little trip, on my way to the Tietê Bus Terminal—the largest bus terminal in Latin America—I had to catch the 5:30 a.m. train from São Paulo. With my suitcase in hand, I descended the escalator to the platform when I noticed a man in front of me do a double take upon realizing I was a travesti. Fear gripped me; I was immediately on high alert, but then I lost sight of him. Imagine my surprise when I found him right behind me on the platform, seemingly awaiting the same train. He started lightly kicking my foot, quite rudely, leaving me confused and anxious about his intentions. Afraid he wanted to start a fight, I noticed he was discreetly attempting to show me something on his phone: his number. He lacked the courage to speak to me, even with a crowd of sleepy strangers at 5:30 a.m.!

Once his intentions were clear, I took down his number and texted him a quick hello. I saw him growing impatient when he didn't receive an immediate reply, then he kicked my foot again, prompting me to check if I had recorded it correctly. I realized I had it wrong. I tried sending the message again, but it wouldn't go through. I attempted to call him so he'd have my number, but that failed too. As we boarded, he whispered "hottie" in my ear before falling silent, staring at his feet for the rest of the ride, unable to even engage in small talk.

As we transferred to the next train, on the escalator he discreetly squeezed my ass. I considered exposing him to the crowd, pulling an Indianarae, but my heavy suitcase made me think twice–it didn't seem worth it. He tried once more to show me his phone number. I played his little game, trying to avoid drawing attention to what I was doing. I wrote it down for a third time, and attempted to call again, still to no luck. I walked away, leaving him staring at the ground, clearly worried someone would see him harass a travesti. Fuck him.

Half an hour later, a message pinged on my phone: "You're gorgeous! I want to see you again!" He lamented that I left him with a huge boner. I told him I had a place to meet later but was on my way to my hometown for now. Then came the classic: "But I don't want to hire you; I want to date you." He couldn't even talk to me in public, yet now he wanted a relationship. Goddess, give me strength, spare me all this nonsense! I replied that for fifty an hour, I would happily date him openly and as often as he wanted.

I know you might think I am a cheap puta, but do you really believe he would pay me more than fifty? You have to understand my side: I wanted him to spend his hard-earned money on me, a form of payback, a reward for my time. Which was why I was going to charge him exactly what he could afford, and then give him poop dick and smear lipstick on his shirt to boot. But right now, I couldn't. I didn't know when I'd be back in São Paulo, so I was mainly testing the waters to see how far he would go. It worked for almost a week, but eventually, he must have grown tired of it–or maybe he blocked my number (I'm devastated).

But the day was far from over, and my trip to my beloved Campinas still had some surprises in store.

40.
THE TRAVESTI'S SAD FATE

I settled into the back of the bus next to the bathroom, hoping to travel in peace. With the bus nearly empty, I placed my bags on the seat beside me. A man emerged from the bathroom, and I noticed his discomfort upon seeing me there–a travesti sitting alone, he must have thought. Instead of returning to his seat at the front, he chose one across the aisle from mine, reclined all the way back, and began stealing glances at me, his face a mix of fear and lust. This silent standoff lasted nearly twenty minutes, leaving me uncertain until I finally decided to meet his gaze. He clearly wanted my body. I patted the empty seat next to me, discreetly inviting him over. He approached, visibly nervous and out of breath. He sat down without a word and pulled out his cock. I guess that's what we're good for. I whispered in his ear: "How much will I get for this?"

"How much do you want?"

"Fifty," I said.

"Thirty," he countered.

Hmm, okay.

I could have tried using a condom, but I have to admit I missed the taste, so I was a little naughty. I started sucking him off right there in the back of that mostly empty bus, hoping no one would feel the need to use the bathroom for a bit. He was so turned on he ended up cumming right away, but the way it happened in the end deserves mention. When a dick goes deep inside one's mouth, it makes it difficult to breathe–the respiratory tract is obstructed, and as the dick comes out, the mucus that floods the canal makes it hard to breathe through the nose. The result is that it's only possible to breathe through your mouth. I was blowing him, which meant I was holding my breath, and from time to time, I stopped to catch my breath and then got back to it. This asshole, however, maybe because he wanted to finish quickly, wanted to be in control of my movements and pushed his dick as deep as possible into my throat, forgetting to let me breathe.

A whore needs to feel empowered to confront this kind of abuse, but that day, I didn't have it in me. I wanted the money, and I didn't even have to ask. My revenge was drooling all over his underwear and slacks, to the point where he needed to go to the bathroom to clean up the mess. Afterward, he returned to his seat at the front of the bus, distancing himself as much as possible from me, avoiding eye contact until the end of the trip. After he came, it's possible he didn't even understand what he felt for me–a freak–perhaps disgust, both for himself and me. This is the tragic fate of the travesti: to evoke desire while simultaneously provoking hatred for awakening that desire. No wonder people kill us, violently attack us; we are living proof that men are not as macho as they believe. What if others found out? Once the thrill is gone, there's no longer any lust to give them the courage to engage with us–no hellos, no goodbyes, not even a smile. We are left with indifference, at best.

41.
POSSIBLE LOVES

That moment when you realize people are staring daggers at you—various glares: hostile, curious, amused, mocking. Maybe they are not looking at you but at the person holding your hand, the one you love. It doesn't matter where you are: on the street, the subway, the bus; in the bathroom; at the movies or the mall. And it doesn't matter who that person is—man, woman, white, Black, fat, thin. The daggers will come all the same. Whoever is with you bears the brunt of those stares; and you, travesti, are solely responsible for those stares. I held off my transition for as long as I could out of love and fear of what the person I loved might experience—fear of them being targeted by the hatred usually aimed at me.

Lesbian, gay, bi—the famous LGB—these labels don't fit us trans people. They're for cis people, for relationships between cis people (cis, as in the opposite of trans: You are on one side or the other, no exceptions). We dismantle these concepts. A cis man who claims to be gay might also say he doesn't date trans men or travestis; the same goes for cis women who identify as lesbians. Not to mention people who say they are straight. It's almost always like that with pretty much everyone, even bisexual cis people. Who is brave enough to admit their attraction to us, to our bodies and existence? T-lovers, chasers, travequeiros, those who only confess their love for us in the dead of night, away from prying eyes. They twist themselves into knots, contorting their desires. It takes courage to acknowledge us as human, to desire us as sexual beings.

I remember a wonderful cis woman I dated who said she never faced those stares when she was with other cis women. But when she dated me, she felt scared for the first time. Those looks were all too familiar to me; I would go crazy if I didn't pretend they were normal. I prefer not to notice them, something cis people might struggle to do. When we walked hand in hand through the city, the looks of confusion, hatred, and derision followed us everywhere. How does one cope? Eventually, she grew more empowered, creating her own armor, and began returning their stares by doubling down on her affection with me in public. It was her way of marking her territory; whenever she touched, kissed, cuddled me more, I knew it was a response to the stares around us.

In another memorable instance, a group of men laughed as I walked by with a woman. One of them shouted in the middle of the farmer's market that if she was with me, it was because she had "never been with a real man." It happened repeatedly–strangers approaching us, asking if we were working together. If I was a travesti, of course I was a prostitute, and any woman with me must be one too, right? Sometimes, people would ignore her entirely, focusing on me, honking, whistling, laughing–reminding us how audacious we were, despite our vulnerability in such a space. To them, our bodies didn't make sense, especially together; our existence made them uncomfortable. Happiness wasn't meant for us; love wasn't something we were entitled to. I became the person who couldn't be introduced to family, the one who took courage to be with.

The truth is, it takes a thick skin to endure all the stares and awkwardness. When their daggers cut not only me but also the person I love, the stakes are much higher. In those moments, I would notice my partner's embarrassment and suddenly become hyperaware of the looks I had long learned to ignore. I would let go of their hand, avoiding any affection in public, leaving my partner unsure whether to thank me or be angry. I would cry, only to remember one of the reasons I entered sex work: As a travesti, this was the only love society had reserved for me—the only kind of love I could experience that wouldn't put anyone else at risk.

42.
SEX WORK AND FREE LOVE

Since I started working as a prostitute a little over a year ago, who has asked me out? Clients, countless ones—my very first one, and so many since that I lost count. But aside from them, no one else has shown interest, which says a lot about the world I navigate. Who in their right mind would want to date a travesti, especially one who's a puta? Some people claim they want to "rescue" me from this life, promising to date me exclusively. "I'll introduce you to my family, take care of your bills," they say. They get excited, aroused sexually by all this talk of salvation, right up until they orgasm; after that, they forget everything they'd promised, all the love. Others approach without the fantasy, more down-to-earth—dare I say, opportunistic. "I'll *let* you keep working," they say (how generous!). "I just want your love and touch when I visit." They spin the same old tired narrative, hoping to get something for nothing—without commitment, without emotional responsibility.

Being a travesti comes with its own unique set of challenges, especially when it comes to love—particularly if you are drawn to cishet men. They embody a standard masculine cisheteronormativity that often seeks to govern us. Luckily, I am bisexual and have dated women too—cis and trans, lesbians and bisexuals—many of whom are activists or deeply engaged in LGBTQ causes. Partners like these take me seriously, holding my hand in public and sharing genuine displays of affection. Our relationships extend beyond the confines of motel rooms and the euphoria of sex. Yet no matter how empowered or determined they are, my status as a sex worker has often posed a challenge for these women. No matter their bravery—essential for liking us, loving us—some preferred to avoid the topic altogether. I have had partners unfollow my blog, too uncomfortable to read the stories they once admired. Others pressed for answers—sometimes subtle, other times more blunt, cutting—asking, "Why do you do it when you could find another job?" Beneath it all, there lingers a question: How long can they sustain a relationship with me, given the stigma attached to my work?

Being a travesti already places me in a taboo category, which is why many of us rely on sex work for survival. Even those who manage to escape this life are still labeled putas. Navigating the overlapping stigmas of our identities and the realities of our relationships is no small feat. It takes immense mental fortitude to handle the pressure that comes from society, our families, and social circles—everything feels threatened simply because of who we are or who we love. Transphobia pushes us away, while prostitution embraces us, and putaphobia only deepens the exclusions we face.

So what do we do? I remember a travesti I dated a decade ago when I was about eighteen. One day at the mall, she slipped her hand from mine, worried about being seen in public. She was afraid of potential consequences, even though I wanted to take it all and hold her hand proudly. Now, I find myself in the opposite position, grappling with whether to allow my partner to stand by me publicly, to show affection, or to introduce me to their family. Each choice feels heavy, with no easy answers.

How do we travestis cope emotionally amid all this stigma, pain, and struggle? We have been raised in a society that champions monogamy, equating love with sex, while simultaneously pushing us into precarious forms of sex work. This society forces us into a relentless cycle, seeing multiple clients each day—each encounter lasting just ten minutes—where they profess love, only to recoil in disgust afterward. Many of us—putas, travestis, both—develop an aversion to sex, even with those we genuinely like. In those relationships, we fear "losing" the few who have the courage to love us, and even in their arms, sex can still feel like an obligation.

It's difficult to navigate this emotional rollercoaster of feelings, fears, and anxieties, while contending with a systematic disregard for emotions. The stigma compels us to play by others' rules, always; we fake romance for a little extra money, even spooning clients in bed if the price is right. Yet there's always a bitter taste left behind at the end of the night. Still, among the constant flow of bodies, we cling to the hope of finding a prince who will accept us, love us genuinely, and take us as we are.

I wonder if free, nonmonogamous love is a possibility for us travestis, especially for the 90 percent of us who are both "travestis" and "prostitutes." The love available to us hardly qualifies as "free love," even with all the clients who propose dating—those men who only allow me to love them in motel rooms, intoxicated by their lust. Yet I believe in the potential to build networks of care that respond to our realities, networks of people who recognize our humanity: an activist love, a love that is both constructed and deconstructed, fostering healthy detachment and challenging traditional notions of love as possessive and exclusive. This could be a creation of our collective heart–one that reconciles love and sex and confronts the violence of being pushed into prostitution while being told that love and sex are the same. It could challenge the romantic expectations that harm us, making us prisoners of those who do not deserve our love, our lust, or our tears. Perhaps this would give us the strength to face our daily challenges, granting us autonomy rooted in our communities, not in the hands of our oppressors. Maybe this would grant us more autonomy to stand up for ourselves, for whomever we seek relations with, and for how we want these relations to be, without having to accept less than we deserve.

For a world where loving a travesti requires no courage at all.

43.
NOT WITH THAT LIPSTICK

They know every pothole in the street, skillfully dodging them when they drive by. Night after night, they cruise the same roads until they finally make up their minds. From a distance, I can spot someone familiar with the neighborhood—a customer who understands how things work. Some shout, "Hey gorgeous," in a mechanical way; if they say the same thing to everyone, it means nothing. Others simply stare, and most pass by without a word, as if the sidewalks are shelves and we are objects on display— no need for them to express what they think or feel. In that atmosphere, I try to catch their attention, stir their desire with a sultry kiss here, a wave there, a playful "Hi, come here."

On this night, three men pulled up to inquire about my price and to "get to know me better." One wanted to know if I could fuck him hard, destroy his asshole; me of all people. No chance could I sustain an erection, especially when the guy did nothing for me. Nope, I am not a walking dick. He understood I couldn't offer him what he wanted, and I didn't deny it. I prefer not to depend on my erection at work, as there's always the risk that nothing will come of it. The others got straight to the point, asking, "How much?" followed by, "I'll take a look around, maybe come back later." Why is it so hard for them to treat us like real people instead of objects? It's incredible how much these interactions can undermine my self-esteem, even on days when I feel good.

But then came the first and only client of the night. He stopped his motorcycle, talked to me while still mounted on top; I was all seductive, speaking in a sexy voice, playfully putting my hand on his crotch while I chatted him up, and he perked up. "How much for a blowjob?"

"For you and just for you, twenty."

"Hmm, but where?"

"Ah, anywhere! But if you're shy, there's a parking lot close by that is a bit darker, or the bushes."

"Let's go to the parking lot then—but what about your lipstick? My wife will kill me if I come home in dirty underwear!"

If there is one thing that pisses me off, it's this. He has a wife at home, waiting, while the travesti is only good for a paid quickie. But I was careful to wipe away my lipstick, using the back of my hand, as he watched.

He went on his motorcycle by himself, ahead of me, paying me in advance to show he was serious. I went on foot, two blocks. When I arrived, he was already there. He told me that there's a sex worker he usually sees, "a woman, not a travesti," but she wasn't on the street today, so he took the opportunity to change things up a bit. Talking was nice, but time is money, so I went for his zipper. His jeans went only halfway down his legs so they didn't get dirty from the floor of the parking lot. A beautiful thick dick, my mouth was watering just imagining my tongue on it—but I slapped a condom on it right away using my mouth, the trick when it's still a bit limp. I started sucking him off while he was standing; I crouched down in my high heels, my legs cramping and sore. His cock was semi-erect at most; harder than mine, which showed no sign of life.

At one point, his dick got hard, he perked up, asked how much more for full service. "Ten more," I said, and out came ten more flying from his pocket. I finally stood up, my calves were already screaming "enough!" and smeared lube on his cock and my hole. He slipped it in from behind, leaning me over his bike, starting to force the door open, trying to slip it in. Nothing. The anal fissure that I sustained on my first day at work reared its ugly head. It was horrible to fuck under these conditions, horrible. At one point, his erection, which was never vigorous to begin with, faded and not even Jesus could resurrect it. He asked me to take the condom off and rub him out. I was unsure; it was the last condom I had. I forgot my bag with a friend. So I told him he wouldn't be able to penetrate me again. He complied, wanting a handjob to get off.

We got to work, and right away he started with the infamous "Do whatever you want to me, touch me anywhere you want." Everyone knows what this means, what he wants is ass play, a knock on his backdoor. Right as I fumbled around that area, I accidently hit his taint, and he muttered, "Go ahead, whatever you want," his semi turning rock hard. "I'm yours, all yours." I was still massaging him. "I can't take it," he couldn't stop ah- and oh-ing, moaning in monosyllables, until he finally came. It happened fast, but I still had to switch hands from exhaustion, and he had to take over in the end while I massaged the rim of his stinky monosyllable—I mean, his ass. He even asked for a light fingering, but I will be damned if I put my little finger in. Be happy I touched the rim, darling. And see if you could trouble yourself to pay for a motel next time: No one should have to fuck standing up.

44.
IF THEY ONLY KNEW

No two clients are the same, neither are any two tricks. From the big dumb guy to the loud aggressive type, each one is human in his own way, and I am interested in all of them. Who are they? Indianarae clarifies, "They're not the soulless villains of popular imaginaries, sick, dirty losers–they are our parents, our brothers, our uncles, our children, our neighbors, all those around us, those that society has raised alongside us." After all, that's what prostitution is all about: Not everyone has easy access to the sex they want, the sex that life made them want. Where else, if not here: Anal, deep throat, the whip, the dildo, rimming, golden showers, even missionary if that's what turns you on. This is a place where a client can be himself, fully, without the mask and the performance required for everyday life. Without the orgasm that I extract from his genitals with the surgical precision of a professional–without that release I provide him–how many of the necessary deceptions would he be able to maintain?

"Rip my asshole open!"
"Rape me!"
"Make me your bitch!"
"Swallow it, all the way!"
"You asked for it, now take it!"
"Say you love me!"
"Cum for me!"

Who people really are, that's what sex workers see. People's nakedness, their barest truest self, is reserved for the true professional, only for those who know how to undress. The fleshy messiness of men isn't often found in books (except this one, of course); it exists naked in our beds, on all fours, begging us to put an end to the farce that is their life, even for a few minutes.

What is this book? Revenge, you might think, but no. These men paid me close to nothing for the sex I performed for them, but they didn't know I was getting a story out of it too. The stories protected me from the naked people in front of me; they saved me from what their nakedness was capable of. I was always the narrator, I was already choosing the right words as the minutes passed, deciding how to frame the scenes I lived, what to focus on, where to put the commas and periods. If my clients knew this, if they knew what they were giving me, if they knew they were, too, selling their souls, perhaps they would prefer to pay me more. A few more reais might have been their best chance of dodging my sharp pen.

ACKNOWLEDGMENTS

This book has many names behind it. For opening the doors and showing me the arts, Amanda Kinah would be one of them. But also Denise Martins, a guide amidst missteps, and Giselly Moraes, for taking care of me. Larissa Pio stood by me through thick and thin. Betânia Santos, for bringing me into the struggle. Indianarae Alves Siqueira and Monique Prada, finally, for believing when perhaps I did not even believe in myself.

AMARA MOIRA is a Brazilian travesti writer and scholar with a PhD in literary criticism and theory. She is the author of *Neca: Romance em Bajubá* (Companhia das Letras, 2024), a groundbreaking monologue written in the vibrant vernacular of travesti sex workers in Brazil. Amara is currently the program coordinator at the Museum of Sexual Diversity in São Paulo, Brazil.

AMANDA DE LISIO is an assistant professor of physical culture, policy, and sustainable development at York University, where she codirects the Critical Trafficking and Sex Work Studies Research Cluster. She is also the editor and cotranslator of *Putafeminista: A Manifesto of Sex Worker Feminism* by Monique Prada (Feminist Press, 2025).

BRUNA DANTAS LOBATO is the author *of Blue Light Hours* (Grove Atlantic, 2024) and the recipient of the 2023 National Book Award in Translated Literature for her translation of *The Wordfs That Remain* by Stênio Gardel (New Vessel Press, 2023). Originally from Natal, Brazil, she lives in Iowa and teaches at Grinnell College.

The Feminist Press publishes books that ignite movements and social transformation. Celebrating our legacy, we lift up insurgent and marginalized voices from around the world to build a more just future.

See our complete list of books at
feministpress.org